COMMUNICATION SKILLS FOR HEALTHIER BOUNDARIES

Communication Skills for Healthier Boundaries

EXPRESS YOUR NEEDS WITHOUT GIVING IN OR BLOWING UP

Dr. LaToya S. Gilmore

ZEITGEIST • NEW YORK

To my cousins

Zeitgeist™

An imprint and division of Penguin Random House LLC

1745 Broadway, New York, NY 10019

zeitgeistpublishing.com

penguinrandomhouse.com

ISBN: 9780593886397

Ebook ISBN: 9798217151417

Book design by Emma Hall

Cover art © by Shutterstock/Alexander Kalina

Author photograph © by Michael Starghill Jr.

Edited by Kim Suarez

Printed in the United States of America on acid-free paper

1st Printing

The authorized representative in the EU for product safety and compliance is Penguin Random House Ireland, Morrison Chambers, 32 Nassau Street, Dublin D02 YH68, Ireland. https://eu-contact.penguin.ie

Contents

Introduction

Do you find it hard to say no to others when you want or need to? Is it difficult for you to communicate in a way that gets the outcomes you desire and deserve? Or do you have so many barriers up that you find yourself isolated from those you care about? If you responded yes to any of these questions, then you're reading the right book at the right time, and I'm glad to have you here!

Perhaps this book is in your hands because you've struggled with asserting yourself or creating boundaries that stick, or maybe you've blown up a time or two—maybe it's a combination of both. This book offers skills and strategies that can be used in everyday life to improve your boundaries—whether that means strengthening them, relaxing them, or simply establishing them where needed.

Communication is key to maintaining healthy relationships and respecting others while ensuring you're taking care of your needs, too. A key step in establishing better boundaries is finding the right way to communicate your needs and the best ways to say yes and no, and you'll learn those skills here.

My personal experiences, along with over 20 years as a behavioral scientist, have equipped me with an immense amount of knowledge related to healthy boundaries. Being a behavioral scientist and practicing clinician does not exempt me from implementing these skills myself—I am known for letting family and friends know when my limits have been reached! I'm happy to be able to share this knowledge so you, too, can establish healthy boundaries across every area of your life, improve relationships, find peace in your decision-making, and become happier and more confident overall.

How to Use This Book

If you feel uncomfortable setting or keeping boundaries, be sure to start with the first section of this book, "Moving Past the Discomfort." This section will deepen your understanding of the guilt and discomfort often associated with setting and keeping boundaries, especially if this is your first time flexing these muscles. You'll be guided through how to improve your ability to identify and work through those uncomfortable emotions with helpful coping skills.

This book is then divided into two parts. Part 1 explores a variety of effective communication tools. Through interactive activities, you will learn what makes each of these tools so helpful and how you can implement them in real life. Part 2 contains real-life scenarios of common issues for people who struggle with communicating and boundary-setting in difficult situations. Here, we'll apply the tools from part 1 to deepen your understanding and discover solutions to the issues described. Although it's beneficial to learn the skills in part 1 before venturing into part 2, this book is intended to be flexible. Personally, I skip through self-help books all the time. There's nothing wrong with going after what you need first. Do what works best for you.

This book includes space for responding to prompts and questions. Feel free to complete these activities in a journal if you prefer or if you want to write more than the space in this book allows. Either way, I recommend getting yourself a journal or notebook to write additional thoughts in, as well as a favorite pen and some sticky notes. You might also choose to underline or highlight specific messages within the book that resonate. The more you reflect on, interact with, and practice the lessons in this book, the stronger your experiences and outcomes will be.

Moving Past the Discomfort

Do you ever wonder why setting and maintaining boundaries is difficult? Perhaps, once boundaries are set or even imagined, that uneasy feeling of guilt or discomfort arises, making it difficult to keep them in place. Feeling uncomfortable, especially if you're a first-time boundary setter, is absolutely normal. This section will explore the four most common feelings that make it hard to communicate, set, and keep boundaries and will offer coping solutions to assist you with facing this kind of discomfort—and releasing it.

Discomfort 1: Anxiety about Establishing Boundaries

I think it's safe to say that for those who had never experienced anxiety before, the global pandemic gave us all a warm introduction to what anxiety is and how unsettling it feels, both mentally and physically. According to the *APA Dictionary of Psychology*, anxiety is "an emotion characterized by apprehension and somatic symptoms of tension in which an individual anticipates impending danger, catastrophe, or misfortune." Impending danger, catastrophe, or misfortune? No wonder there's hesitation with establishing boundaries if this uncomfortable emotion is present!

Anxiety can be debilitating and terrifying. Its presence can zap our motivation instantly. We become anxious because we don't know what to expect. Or we fear the worst will happen. With regard to boundaries, this might look like *If I say no, will they get mad? Will they think I'm selfish? If I don't do this for them, they may never ask me for anything again and they may not be there for me when I need them.*

Anxiety comes from a need to control outcomes. We project into the future to ensure we'll *know* results—how it ends. Knowing seems to create a sense of peace because we feel more prepared. But are we? Anxiety related to boundary creation comes from fear of not knowing how those we're implementing the boundaries with will respond. We are afraid: *If I tell them what I really think, I will lose them. It's been this way all this time; I think it's too late to say something about it.*

COPING SOLUTION 1: REPLACE THOSE IRRATIONAL THOUGHTS!

Think of anxiety as a balloon we need to deflate. This balloon is filled with irrational thoughts. Let's use facts like sharp pins to pop it. Facts might include the following:

* *I can't control whether they get mad, but I can make sure I'm listening to my needs and taking care of them.*

* *Taking care of myself is not selfish.*

* *Even though I'm not available to help them today, I can assist on Wednesday.*

* *I care about showing up authentically in my relationships.*

* *It's never too late to begin asserting my boundaries.*

Think of a situation that's filling you with anxiety. Are there facts that strengthen your resolve? Write them down in and around the balloon. Then, write your favorites on sticky notes and post them somewhere you will see them often. Reminding yourself of these facts can help you stay calm and think rationally when you need to stand your ground.

Discomfort 2: Threat of Loneliness If a Boundary Is Created

We are created to connect. According to author Brené Brown, "At the heart of loneliness is the absence of meaningful social interaction . . . Belonging is essential to our well-being." Loneliness threatens boundary creation because of a perceived fear of isolation. It may manifest as *I'll go along just to belong.* Or it could be accompanied with a thought like *The possibility of isolation or separation isn't worth it (the boundary).*

Let's think about our relationships for a minute. Do you have a close friend or family member who means the world to you but makes you feel as if your relationship with them is contingent on certain factors? Maybe they do all the talking and never listen to you? Or maybe they have views or lifestyle habits that you don't agree with, but you go along with them in the interest of keeping the peace? Relationships built on these kinds of contingencies can deplete our energy and leave us feeling like we can't be ourselves. In extreme circumstances, they can even result in formation of unhealthy habits, illicit behaviors, and damage to our emotional and physical well-being.

COPING SOLUTION 2: AFFIRM YOUR VALUE

Even though we all want to be accepted and loved by others, it's important to be true to ourselves, too. Not showing up in spaces as our authentic self, with an ability to communicate our needs, can also foster loneliness. Brown offsets her earlier comment by adding, "We have to belong to ourselves as much as we need to belong to others. Any belonging that asks us to betray ourselves is not true belonging."

Using affirmations can aid in overcoming the threat of loneliness and is a great tool to apply to any situation. Here are some examples:

* *I know my view of this may go against the grain; I'm OK with being different.*

* *I am capable of building community.*

* *I deserve to surround myself with people who value me.*

* *I don't have to settle, and I won't.*

* *I don't have to do something/believe in something just because someone else wants me to.*

Can you think of some affirmations that speak to your ability to connect with others? Write these affirmations down. Set them as your background on your phone or computer. Let them remind you of your worth as well as your desire to be authentic to yourself and others.

Discomfort 3: Guilt after Imposing a Strong Boundary

How often have you had feelings of guilt after you implemented a strong boundary? Maybe your capacity was reached and you reacted with a statement or action, but then you thought, *Was that too harsh?* Or have you ever felt bad, like you've done something wrong for standing up for yourself, even though your communication was respectful to both you and the other person?

Where does this come from? I suspect its origins can be found in deficits with identifying and prioritizing our needs. Many of us have grown accustomed to placing others' needs, wants, and desires before our own, to the point that once we get around to using healthy boundaries, it's so foreign that we feel like we're doing something wrong or bad. And that's not fair to us! We deserve to protect our own values, wishes, and limitations as much as we show concern for those of others.

COPING SOLUTION 3: USE ASSERTIVE COMMUNICATION

Assertive communication is a cornerstone of healthy boundaries that we'll discuss in greater length throughout this book. What it means is the ability to advocate for our own wants, needs, and feelings while also respecting and hearing the needs of others.

Let's say you've established a firm boundary that you will take lunch and other breaks at work instead of working through them, and then a nonessential meeting is called during that time. Here's a response example using assertive communication: "I see that a meeting was scheduled when I'm off for lunch. I need to take this time, but I'll get the notes when I return."

You are acknowledging that it is important to honor your boundary; you're also recognizing it is your responsibility to seek the details from this meeting. This respects both views, as you are holding yourself accountable while honoring your boundary.

Discomfort 4: Feelings of Insecurity

When we're insecure, we may feel uncertain about a boundary that we put in place, thus weakening its strength, because we're unsure about ourselves in general. This is when we waive the boundary, "just this time," and then again next time. We fold. We regress. We allow undesirable behaviors or treatment from others to continue unchallenged without advocating for ourselves. We no longer prioritize our self-care, and with that wane the initial confidence and determination it took to establish the boundary. Insecurity makes our boundaries penetrable, creating discomfort for us.

This is so frustrating. After all, we created these boundaries for a reason. And when we go to all the trouble of gathering the courage to create a boundary, what a painful cycle it must be to then back off from that boundary and be left feeling exactly the way we did before: stepped on, pushed around, or silenced. Let's do something about that.

COPING SOLUTION 4: EXPLORE YOUR STRENGTHS

Being aware of our strengths helps build confidence. So, make a list of your strengths. If this is challenging, google a list of positive attributes and think about which of those apply to you. Once you have a list, try turning those strengths into short sentences: *I am adventurous. I am curious. I am caring. I am disciplined. I am funny. I am lighthearted. I am honest. I am persistent.*

Then ask yourself, *What am I good at? What do I enjoy doing? What have I found success in?* Make a list of these strengths, too.

Revisit this solution often! As you make a routine of exploring and acknowledging your strengths, you'll build your confidence by shifting your focus from areas of deficit to your gifts and assets. Just remember, thoughts are powerful, and how you view yourself really matters!

Setting Expectations and Tips for Success

Because awareness is an early step toward change, I hope you realize that you are already one step closer to improving your ability to establish boundaries that guide you toward the life and healthier relationships you want.

Before you transition into the next part of this book, I'd like to offer a few strategies borrowed from fellow educator Camille Kirksey:

STOP. Take a break from reading.

REFLECT. Think about what you've read so far.

COLLECT. Collect and write down the thoughts that come to you.

With this book, resist the urge to go without stopping or slowing down. This book is not a race. My goal for you is to allow true transformation to take place, and absorption is key to that. Allow the concepts and skills to really sink in.

Not that you require my permission—the book is yours!—but it's OK if you feel the need to highlight, underline, or go back and reread sections. After all, interaction and repetition assist with retention.

Consequently, retention leads to change, as you challenge former mindsets and unlearn limiting beliefs and restricting frameworks that have masked a portion of who you are and what you have access to. Imagine freedom to live confidently connected, void of haunting shame or worry! And if you're accustomed to self-criticism or putting others first, this will be an adjustment, so as you go, try to treat yourself like you would a good friend.

Also, remember that emotions are purposeful. Your feelings are signals that inform you of what you need or want or both. Even distressing emotions are purposeful: They warn and protect you. They also guide you and help you release what you were never meant to hold within.

During breaks in my workday, I usually gravitate into the room with the most sunlight shining through the windows and take a seat for a few minutes. I sit with my eyes closed and chin directed upward, inviting the warmth of the sun to rest on my skin, to recharge me before moving on to the next task. That's the kind of engagement this book calls for. Soak it up—every section—before moving on to the next. Your intentionality will pay off.

PART 1

Effective Communication Skills

In the next five chapters, we'll explore the following communication categories: assertive communication, nonverbal communication, empathy, listening, and respect. These foundational areas can promote and enhance effective boundary-setting. In fact, in working with therapy clients for over two decades, I've found these concepts essential to achieving and maintaining healthier connections with self and others. I like to consider them the pillars of effective communication. Whether it's within romantic relationships or with family, friends, colleagues, or the community at large, honing your communication skills will only improve the overall quality of your life. Learning these skills is the first step, but daily practice—repetition—is the real trick to mastering them.

CHAPTER 1

Assertive Communication

Assertive communication is the ability to advocate for yourself while also respecting the needs of others. It includes not dismissing yourself or passively giving in, which can foster learned helplessness or a victim mindset. Conversely, it's also not about aggressively defending your point of view in a manner that results in reactions you later regret. Assertive communication allows you to speak with a confidence that affirms what is of value and importance to you without demeaning another.

Grounded in Knowing

The purpose of learning this skill is to be grounded in knowing what matters to you the most—your core values. You'll have the chance to consider what is of the highest priority to *you*. No one else. For the sake of this activity, let's define *values* as the worth, usefulness, or importance attached to something. *Core values* will therefore be defined as the most central worth, usefulness, or importance of something to us. They're the "why" of who we are and what we do.

WHAT YOU WILL LEARN

* The fundamentals of core values

* What your core values are

WHAT YOU WILL NEED

* 10 minutes

* Pen

INSTRUCTIONS

1. Using the list provided, identify at least five attributes you consider to be your core values. This list isn't exhaustive, so feel free to add your own.

2. Write down your core values here.

_____

_____

_____

_____

_____

3. Revisit this list often. It can be used to inform your boundaries in many ways, which we'll explore later, as well as how you show up in the world.

Accountability	Dignity	Harmony	Nature	Self-improvement
Accuracy	Directness	Health	Nurturing	Service
Achievement	Diversity	Home	Openness	Significance
Acknowledgment	Efficiency	Honesty	Optimism	Simplicity
Adventure	Elegance	Hope	Orderliness	Spirituality
Aesthetics	Empowerment	Hospitality	Participation	Spontaneity
Altruism	Encouragement	Humility	Partnership	Sportsmanship
Ambition	Environment	Humor	Patience	Success
Authenticity	Equality	Inclusion	Patriotism	Teamwork
Balance	Excellence	Independence	Peace	Time
Beauty	Fairness	Initiative	Performance	Tradition
Belonging	Faith	Integrity	Personal power	Transparency
Career	Family	Intuition	Productivity	Trust
Caring	Focus	Job stability	Recognition	Truthfulness
Collaboration	Forgiveness	Joy	Relaxation	Understanding
Commitment	Free-spiritedness	Kindness	Reliability	Uniqueness
Community	Freedom	Knowledge	Resourcefulness	Vision
Compassion	Friendship	Laughter	Respect	Vitality
Confidence	Fun	Leadership	Responsibility	Vulnerability
Connection	Generosity	Learning	Rest	Wealth
Contribution	Giving back	Legacy	Risk-taking	Well-being
Courage	Grace	Leisure	Romance	
Creativity	Gratitude	Love	Safety	
Curiosity	Groundedness	Loyalty	Self-discipline	
Determination	Growth	Motivation	Self-expression	

Cultivating Confidence

One of the most empowering perspectives to have is an understanding of who you are and the characteristics you possess. These are your gifts. Now that you've identified your core values, this knowledge can reinforce the strength of any boundary you set by connecting your boundaries with a purpose. Identifying your core values also serves to explore your strengths. By owning your strengths, you cultivate confidence. Confidence reinforces your boundaries, increasing the likelihood that you'll adhere to them and require others to do the same.

WHAT YOU WILL LEARN

* How core values strengthen confidence

* How confidence reinforces your boundaries

* How boundaries with meaning behind them are stronger

* Personal benefits associated with your core values

WHAT YOU WILL NEED

* 10 to 15 minutes

* Your core values list from Grounded in Knowing (page 18)

* Pen

INSTRUCTIONS

1. List your core values below.

------

2. Think about and journal on why your core values reside at the center of who you are. It doesn't have to be a long entry, but reflect mindfully as you grow in the confidence of resting in who you are. Explain why you chose each core value. Use the following examples as a guide.

* REST: *Rest is a priority for me and core value because when I'm rested, my mind, body, and soul feel renewed. Rest helps me focus, so I make fewer mistakes. This is the reason I choose not to bring work home. Rest also physically energizes me and increases my productivity during work hours.*

* FAMILY TIME: *I value time with family. It's sacred and I am very protective of it, which is why I turn on Do Not Disturb during non-work hours.*

* BALANCE: *Even though I work extremely hard, there's a purpose. I do it so I can travel more. I enjoy learning about new cultures and trying new cuisine and experiences. This allows me to maintain the balance I want in my life.*

* Core value and reasoning: _____

_____

_____

_____

* Core value and reasoning: _____

_____

_____

_____

_____

* Core value and reasoning: _____

_____

_____

_____

_____

* Core value and reasoning: _____

_____

_____

_____

_____

* Core value and reasoning: _____

_____

_____

_____

_____

3. Reflect on your responses. Do you see how your boundaries gain meaning and strength when you consider how they honor your core values? Do you think you can more easily uphold these boundaries because of their connection to your greatest priorities?

SKILL 3

Assertively Advocating

Now that you've identified how your core values impact some of your boundaries and how these boundaries gain strength by their connection to your priorities, let's explore the cornerstones of assertive communication. Think of being assertive as the harmonious blend of just enough firmness mixed with flexibility. This activity will help you figure out what kind of communication you tend to use, then it'll equip you with assertive communication components you can use right away in boundary-setting situations.

WHAT YOU WILL LEARN

* Components of assertive communication

* What assertive communication is not

* How to communicate assertively

* How core values guide boundaries

WHAT YOU WILL NEED

* 20 minutes

* Pen

INSTRUCTIONS

1.   Read these four helpful tips for assertive communication:

   * THINK ABOUT IT. Why can't you help that person move on Saturday? Oh, that's right, it's because you had a prior commitment and you want to refrain from making their priority yours. Give yourself permission to carefully consider the outcome you want in the given situation.

   * GET TO THE POINT. State your case clearly and directly: "I can't help you move Saturday. I already have plans." Sometimes the boundary is

as simple as a response of "No," with or without an explanation. Your no is enough.

* MIND YOUR NONVERBALS. Generally, good eye contact is considered respectful and displays confidence. Posture, gestures, and expressions also communicate for us. Consider how you can relax your posture by uncrossing your arms or taking your hands off your hips. Are your facial expressions displaying anger or anxiety? Be mindful of these nonverbal cues.

* CHECK YOUR TONE. Take a deep breath, and use a calm, clear voice to express yourself. When you're feeling stepped on or not heard, it can be tempting to elevate your voice to get your message across. Unfortunately, yelling shuts down the opportunity for a helpful dialogue, puts the listener on the defense, and sets you up for feelings of regret.

2. Now stop and think about your current approach to communication. Are you reluctant to ask for what you need or hesitant to say no? Do you show outward aggression when your boundaries are tested? Write about this. If you're not sure, get feedback from those who know you well._____

_____

_____

_____

_____

3. Commit to listening closely. When we show interest, others feel like they are heard, even if the outcome isn't what they want. Here's an example: "Is there anyone else you can ask? I can't help, but I believe John's college-age son is looking for work."

4. Compromise if you can and want to. "I can't help you move this Saturday, but I can stop by for a few hours on Sunday afternoon." This compromise allows you to help on your terms.

5. Practice using these skills in front of a mirror, especially if you have an upcoming decision to make that involves asserting your boundaries.

A Note on Passive-Aggressive Behavior

Have you ever heard the term *passive-aggressive* used to describe someone? According to the *APA Dictionary of Psychology*, passive-aggressive action is characterized by "behavior that is seemingly non-offensive, accidental, or neutral but indirectly displays an unconscious aggressive motive." If you can picture this or even relate, you may understand the mindset behind it. Passive-aggressive behavior can result from an inability or unwillingness to assert oneself directly or because of pent-up frustration from continued negative interactions with a person or situation. This book can help with that by building the skills it takes to express yourself clearly in any situation. You *can* do this. Keep reading to strengthen those muscles.

Passing on Passivity

Have you ever found yourself either self-sacrificing or self-sabotaging in the face of a boundary dilemma? A person self-sabotages by prioritizing others over themselves. Those of us who struggle in this area may find ourselves taken advantage of, either maliciously or unintentionally, by people unaware of our unspoken needs. Passive communicators may be soft-spoken, avoid eye contact, and/or lack confidence. This skill will focus on the traits of passive communication and how to avoid falling into its trap.

WHAT YOU WILL LEARN

* What passive communication is

* Characteristics of a passive communicator

* How to avoid self-sabotaging

* More assertive ways of responding

WHAT YOU WILL NEED

* 10 to 15 minutes

* Pen

INSTRUCTIONS

1. From the table on page 27, read the following requests (column 1) and examples of passive responses (column 2). In column 3, write down a more assertive response to each request.

2. Can you think of some recent instances when your response did not align with your wishes? If so, journal some ways you can respond more assertively next time.

---

3. Read over your assertive responses, and reflect on how responding this way will make you feel.

_____

_____

_____

REQUEST	PASSIVE RESPONSE AND THOUGHT	ASSERTIVE RESPONSE
I need someone to drive my sick kid home from school and watch them while I work. Can you help?	"I have some things to do, but I guess I can help." (*How am I going to do this?*)	Example: "Oh no, I'm sorry they aren't feeling well. Unfortunately, I can't help—I have some things to take care of."
Call me tonight.	"I will." (*I wanted to go to bed early.*)	
I know you're busy, but I have to tell you this story.	"OK." (*Her stories are never quick.*)	
I have to touch your belly. You're getting so big!	"Haha, sure." (*I feel totally violated.*)	
Ooh, yum! (grabs French fry off your plate)	"Oh, help yourself." (*I hate when people do that.*)	

SKILL 5

Beyond Blowing Up

Aggressive communication aims to get one's own needs and wants met but dismisses others. This egocentric form of communicating lacks reciprocity and consideration for others and their feelings. It's often marked by the use of criticism, humiliation, disrespect, poor listening skills, interruptions, and an unwillingness to compromise. Ironically, the control a person is seeking through aggression actually proves the opposite—they're out of control. If you can relate, don't despair. We never stop growing, and change is a choice that is in our power.

WHAT YOU WILL LEARN

* What aggressive communication looks like

* How to de-escalate an aggressive response

WHAT YOU WILL NEED

* 10 to 15 minutes

* Pen

INSTRUCTIONS

1. Take a reflective pause. Do you ever become aggressive in your communication? With one particular person? With everyone? In a specific situation? Consider this honestly, without judging yourself. Write down your findings.

    ----

2. If you've identified a person (or more than one) or situation that triggers you to communicate aggressively, think about why you might react this way. Are you feeling threatened? Violated? Misunderstood? Something else? Write about this, too.

    ----

3. Consider what your aggressive response typically looks like. Is it direct? Indirect? Expressed loudly or with expletives? Physical?

----

4. Now, considering the tools you've learned in this chapter, think about what you can say or do to express yourself in a more assertive (but less aggressive) way. If you feel your aggression is possibly being triggered by something, write about how you might clear the air or otherwise deal with that trigger. One good way to disarm a trigger is to STOP: Stop, Take a breath, Observe, and Proceed. You can even say "stop" to yourself, giving you the pause to consider how you really want to respond.

----

5. Finally, be empowered moving forward. It takes practice to change old habits, but increased self-awareness is the first step. You're in the right place, doing the right things.

   If your aggression is triggered by someone who is emotionally abusive or unavailable, is selfish or self-absorbed, is constantly irritable or harsh, or lacks empathy, consider the following:

   * Remember that it takes two to argue. Refuse to engage and step away. ("I will not argue this point. Let's talk later.")

   * Say something to de-escalate and implicitly point out their behavior. ("Did I do/say something to offend you?")

   * Get help. Individual, family, and couples therapy can be beneficial in breaking these cycles (see Resources, page 146).

   * See the sidebar "Rigid Boundaries in Response to Abuse" (page 55).

CHAPTER 2

Communication Tools and Methods

This chapter explores how boundaries are communicated using various methods. Whether it's spoken, written, texted, or posted on social media, we sometimes have to set boundaries, and there are good (and not-so-good!) ways to do it. We'll revisit the five tools from chapter 1 and explore how they can be used via different communication methods. The goal is retention and application—a.k.a. practice—so using tools like boundaries becomes muscle memory. For readers who learn by doing, feel free to revisit the previous sections as you navigate through this chapter.

Connecting Strengths and Values

Have you ever thought to ask someone close to you what they see as your strengths? This is a great way to learn more about yourself. How you are perceived by others doesn't define you, but chances are good that your biggest supporters have a pretty good read on what makes you tick. Having a clear depiction of who you are is a solid foundation to lay healthy boundaries on. When you know your value, you're more likely to hold firm to what you want, need, and deserve.

WHAT YOU WILL LEARN

* Importance of self-awareness

* Your strengths as seen by others

* How your strengths inform your core values and boundaries

WHAT YOU WILL NEED

* 5 minutes to read, plus time to speak with others

* Your core values list from Grounded in Knowing (page 18)

* Pen

INSTRUCTIONS

1. Ask at least three close friends, trusted colleagues, and/or family members to share what they value about you or view as your strengths. Fill in their answers in the columns below.

TRUSTED PERSON #1	
TRUSTED PERSON #2	
TRUSTED PERSON #3	

2. Think about how these positive qualities might manifest in your core values and, as such, in your boundaries. Take out your list of core values and review them. Are there any revelations—maybe a core value you hadn't considered before? Or common themes among the responses? For example, if your trusted people seem to agree that you are a loyal friend, maybe that explains why relationships are a core value and why you make boundaries to protect your time with loved ones.

3. Let this goodness fill you up. We often have blind spots and find it difficult to accept the compliments we receive. Allow their responses to serve as verifiable facts of who you are.

Written Boundaries

Some people find it more comfortable to write or type a boundary, as opposed to verbalizing it. The tricky part is creating a message that conveys your needs assertively, without aggression or passivity. Whether it's by electronic means or the traditional pen-to-paper format, this tool can help you become confident expressing your wants and needs in writing. You'll be able to sift through the emotions associated with the need for the boundary and get right to the point in a way that respects both you and the recipient.

WHAT YOU WILL LEARN

* Benefits of written boundaries

* How to assess your writing for tone

* How to communicate healthy and effective written boundaries

WHAT YOU WILL NEED

* 30 to 40 minutes

* Your core values list from Grounded in Knowing (page 18)

* Pen

INSTRUCTIONS

1. Think about a boundary that you need to set. Perhaps you need to say no to a request, or maybe a colleague is demanding more of you than is fair. Write it below.

2. What do you want to say? Write down your message exactly the way you want to say it. Only you will see this, so don't hold back. Release any judgmental thoughts that may come up, and allow the words to flow onto the page.

3. Read over what you just wrote. Read it out loud. How does it sound? Aggressive? Passive? Just right? Does it meet the criteria for Assertively Advocating (page 23)? Write down your thoughts.

---

4. If your message was aggressive or passive, take a deep breath and rewrite the boundary using assertive communication.

---

5. Think about your new response. Does it say what you want to say? What, if anything, do you think needs adjustment? How would you feel sending this message?

---

6. If you feel like you can, share this message with someone you really trust. Ask for their feedback. If you're confident that the message is clear and assertive, feel free to send it to the recipient.

Here are some helpful guidelines for writing an assertive message expressing a boundary:

* WATCH THE TONE. It isn't what you say but how it's said. The tone of your message matters.

* KEEP IT SIMPLE. Focus on the purpose of your message, keeping it as brief and clear as possible.

* AVOID BLAMING. Instead of accusing ("You give me all your work to do"), use an "I" statement to express how you feel because of their actions. ("I feel overwhelmed by the amount of work/tasks already assigned to me.")

* STATE YOUR BOUNDARY. "I've got a backlog of work, too, so I'm no longer able to help you with your projects." No apology, no aggression.

* SHARE A SOLUTION. If desired, sharing a solution could be helpful. ("If another project is assigned to me, I plan on speaking to the manager. Have you considered this?")

Boundaries in Texts, Emails, and Group Chats

For most of us, technology has permeated every crevice of our daily lives. Cell phones, computers, GPS—it's everywhere and it's always *on*. It's nearly impossible to avoid. And it's really difficult to compartmentalize—after all, we've been programmed to pull the phone from our pocket at the sound of a random ping, even when we're otherwise occupied. So, what can we do to take back time and space for ourselves? I'll show you.

WHAT YOU WILL LEARN

* How to implement effective boundaries within electronic communication

* How core values benefit from effective boundaries

WHAT YOU WILL NEED

* 10 to 15 minutes

* Your core values list from Grounded in Knowing (page 18)

* Pen

INSTRUCTIONS

1. Read the following three scenarios.

2. For each scenario, write down what your response might be. (The first one is offered as an example.)

3. Identify and write down which values are being prioritized (like in the example), especially considering your core values.

Scenario 1

You get a text from a friend saying, "Hey, call me!" but you're just getting home from work and need to decompress from the day.

RATIONALIZATION AND EXAMPLE RESPONSE: You're not obligated to respond immediately to anyone if it's a non-emergency situation. If you desire to respond, here's one way:

"Hi, I'm just getting home. I'll give you a call in a few hours after I settle in."

VALUES PRIORITIZED: rest, self-respect, well-being, balance, authenticity, connection

Scenario 2

You've been awaiting an email from someone regarding a prospective work opportunity for three weeks; you were originally told you'd hear from them within one week. You're becoming anxious and annoyed.

RATIONALIZATION: Your feelings should not be dismissed or ignored. Instead of sitting around wondering if they'll contact you, reach out with a follow-up. It's empowering.

YOUR RESPONSE: _____

_____

_____

VALUES PRIORITIZED: _____

_____

_____

Scenario 3

You're a member of a workplace group chat. Sometimes it's fun, but you've been extremely busy lately, and you're being overwhelmed by a constant barrage of incoming messages that are irrelevant and disruptive.

YOUR RESPONSE: _____
_____
_____

VALUES PRIORITIZED: _____
_____
_____

RATIONALIZATION: Please note that not checking a group chat during a strenuous workweek can be considered a healthy boundary on its own. This is a form of unplugging, and it is self-care.

Boundaries and Social Media

Have you ever found yourself scrolling for what you thought was a few minutes, but in actuality a few hours passed? How did you lose track of time? Blocking time on a calendar to add structure and boundaries to social media use can create parameters that help you maintain focus and avoid accidental loss of time. This does require intentionality and discipline, but it's an achievable and worthwhile goal, especially if you feel like social media is controlling you.

WHAT YOU WILL LEARN

* How to limit social media use

* Benefits of time blocking/ scheduling

* Social media choices that enhance, not detract from, your well-being

WHAT YOU WILL NEED

* 45 minutes, plus time to test the schedule

* Your core values list from Grounded in Knowing (page 18)

* Cell phone (optional)

* Calendar (planner or app)

* Pen and highlighters (optional)

INSTRUCTIONS

1. Fill in your calendar or calendar app for the next 30 days with every meeting, appointment, community service project, trip, class, workshop, after-school pickup/drop-off, and so on. You may find it helpful to color-code tasks for different categories.

2. Take a look at your blocked schedule. Next, think about how much time you'd like to spend on social media and when. During breaks? In the evening? Once identified, mark those "appointments" on your calendar, too.

3. Since the goal is to transition from passively scrolling to deliberately scheduling your time, consider now how you want to use your social media time. Ask yourself,

   Do I enjoy the content that pops up on my feed?

   Is it time to disengage from certain accounts or sites?

   Could I benefit from turning on the app's limits?

4. Make any needed changes to your accounts to optimize the content you receive.

5. Try this new system for a week. Then ask yourself,

   How's this working for me?

   How do I feel now that I'm blocking my social media time?

   Is there anything I need to change? Amount of time? Time of day? Content?

6. Implement any changes that will help you maintain healthy boundaries with the seductive allure of social media!

Boundaries and Self-Care

Sometimes the person we need to implement boundaries with the most is ourselves. Do you know when to put your phone down? Rest? Say no? Recharge with those you love? Venture out in nature? Honoring our internal boundaries can be challenging because we're the only ones holding ourselves accountable. Self-care, the practice of prioritizing one's own overall well-being, includes any intentional action taken to maintain physical, mental, and emotional health. Healthy boundaries are a vital form of self-care because they help us avoid burnout. Let's create some.

WHAT YOU WILL LEARN

* Fundamentals, categories, and benefits of self-care

* How to create healthy boundaries as a form of self-care

WHAT YOU WILL NEED

* 20 to 30 minutes

* Pen

INSTRUCTIONS

1. Respond to the following prompts:

   * **Physical** self-care measures I can take include (examples: get better rest, exercise, eat better, quit unhealthy habits, use insurance benefits to access needed health care resources):

   _____

   _____

   _____

*   **Emotional** self-care measures I can take include (examples: say no when needed, address unhealthy relationships, seek therapy/support):

    _____

    _____

    _____

    _____

*   **Spiritual** self-care measures I can take include (examples: lean into your higher power, volunteer, read spiritual materials, gather with a faith community):

    _____

    _____

    _____

    _____

*   **Professional** self-care measures I can take include (examples: take lunch, stretch hourly, set work boundaries/say no, take time off/mental health days):

    _____

    _____

    _____

    _____

2. Next, look over the self-care measures you just listed and make them more specific.

    (Example: "To get better rest, dim lights and turn off screens 30 minutes before bed and listen to a calming app, nature sounds, or music.")

    _____

    _____

    _____

    _____

3. Now, list any barriers you have to implementing self-care practices regularly. Consider and write possible solutions. (Example: "Barrier to exercise: My feet hurt. Solution: Choose a low-impact activity, like swimming, yoga, or stationary biking.")

4. Finally, set an intention to follow through on measures that apply to each category this week. Write down each intention. (Example: "This week, I will turn screens off 30 minutes before bed, say no to lunch with my needy friend and instead go for a solo walk on my lunch break, and read up on some spiritual affirmations.")

* PHYSICAL INTENTION:

* EMOTIONAL INTENTION:

* SPIRITUAL INTENTION:

* PROFESSIONAL INTENTION:

CHAPTER 3

Listening to Learn

When we hear the word *communication*, many of us instinctively think about speaking or writing. On the other end of that conversation, however, is (hopefully) someone listening. When you're the listener, what you hear tells you what a person is experiencing. What you hear will also determine if a boundary needs to be established. Good listening skills are vital; in fact, I think we all can benefit from sharpening them occasionally. This chapter will explore the various listening skills that can help us respond for the benefit of ourselves and others.

Empathetic Listening

An empathetic listener is the ideal listener. They aren't distracted by their own agenda or inclined to interrupt you. Nor do they assume they know what you need, sharing unsolicited advice or anecdotes. And they're not the person who tries to offer platitudes when you are suffering a loss. An active empathetic listener does more than hear; they show that they honor how the other person *feels*. You don't have to be a licensed therapist to acquire this skill; all that's required is a desire to be a listener who actively seeks to understand.

WHAT YOU WILL LEARN

* What empathetic listening is (and is not)

* Ways to demonstrate empathetic listening

* Your areas of strength in listening

* Opportunities for improvement in listening

WHAT YOU WILL NEED

* 15 minutes

* Pen

INSTRUCTIONS

1. Rate the following statements as honestly as possible on a scale of 1 to 5, which will help gauge how well you sense, process, and respond to others who are speaking.

2. If you answered honestly, a higher score (with more 4s and 5s) indicates a higher level of empathy and engagement in listening. But even a lower score is OK, because empathetic listening is an acquirable skill. We can keep these statements in mind and use them when we listen to others. Either way, we can all benefit from improving our listening skills—let's carry on!

	NEVER	NOT OFTEN	OCCASIONALLY	FREQUENTLY	ALMOST ALWAYS
I am sensitive to what others say.	1	2	3	4	5
I can usually sense what others are implying even when they aren't saying it.	1	2	3	4	5
I believe I understand the way others feel.	1	2	3	4	5
I try to assess a message beyond the words (tone, body language, etc.).	1	2	3	4	5
I make a point of reinforcing what others say by circling back to their words.	1	2	3	4	5
I refer to people by name during conversations with them.	1	2	3	4	5
I refer back to previous conversations with others when I speak with them.	1	2	3	4	5
I use verbal and physical acknowledgments to show listening and understanding.	1	2	3	4	5
I respond affirmatively to worthwhile comments, messages, and ideas.	1	2	3	4	5
I ask questions when I don't understand something.	1	2	3	4	5
People have told me they think I'm a good listener.	1	2	3	4	5

Reflective Listening

In reflective listening, the listener repeats the speaker's idea back to them to confirm it was understood correctly. Empathy is necessary here because it requires you to repeat their message as *they* gave it. Think about looking in a mirror. It displays exactly what it faces. It doesn't add to it, nor does it take anything away. So how do we listen reflectively? By listening with a nonjudgmental perspective, avoiding assumptions, and asking questions when they're done speaking.

WHAT YOU WILL LEARN

* What reflective listening is

* Benefits of reflective listening

* How to use reflective listening

WHAT YOU WILL NEED

* 20 minutes

* Pen

INSTRUCTIONS

1. In the following scenario, choose the response that best illustrates reflective listening.

    SPEAKER: "I'm baffled why I didn't get a better raise. I worked overtime, met all the objectives, and covered my colleague's desk when he was out on leave."

    RESPONSE 1: "That's not fair! You should have gotten a big raise!"

    RESPONSE 2: "So, you don't understand why you didn't get compensated fairly for the extra work you did this year. Is that right?"

    RESPONSE 3: "That happened to me, too, when I worked there."

2. While all these responses are supportive in their own way, response 2 is the one that best illustrates reflective listening.

    Now it's your turn. Read what the speaker is saying on the left, then write a response that demonstrates reflective listening on the right.

SPEAKER	YOUR RESPONSE
My mom said she doesn't want to come over for dinner. I can't figure out whether she's mad at me or just doesn't like my cooking.	
I can't believe Juan told me about the party he was having but didn't invite me. Why would he do that?	

Reflective listening gives the speaker the opportunity to verify the accuracy of their own words and ideas. It also reduces misunderstandings for both the speaker and the listener. The next time you engage in conversation, look for opportunities to use reflective listening. As you do, think about any barriers that may come up for you. Do you have trouble doing this? If so, try the following to enhance your reflective listening skills:

1. Listen closely to the speaker's message.

2. Think about their message. What exactly did they say?

3. Reflect the message back to the speaker without embellishment.

4. Get confirmation that you properly understood the message—or didn't. If the speaker repeats their message in different words to clarify themselves, listen closely again and acknowledge if you understand them.

Appreciative Listening

With appreciative listening, you give someone or something your undivided attention because you're personally invested. This type of listening is about enjoyment. It's also an aspect of self-care because you're engaging in an activity that renews you. Whether it's music, theater, a podcast, a stage play, a film, or a show, it resonates with you, and you learn more about yourself because of it. Electing to pause to care for yourself through enjoyment is a healthy boundary as much as using the word *no*.

WHAT YOU WILL LEARN

* What appreciative listening is

* How appreciative listening is a form of self-care and a healthy boundary

* How appreciative listening makes you feel

WHAT YOU WILL NEED

* 30 to 60 minutes

* Something you enjoy listening to

* Pen

INSTRUCTIONS

1. Find something or someone you enjoy listening to, put this book down, and go enjoy it. Then come back here.

2. Write about your experience. Include anything notable regarding how you felt while listening, what your thoughts were during this time, and how it left you feeling afterward.

Comfortable Silence

Silence in conversation allows us to hear requests, needs, and the emotion in what is being said. It can help us gather feedback and identify solutions. Being silent and mindful in our environment helps usher us into reflection, tuning out other opinions that can clutter our mind. When only our internal voice remains, silence has the power to center us. Reveal. Relieve. But it can also create discomfort in some. The experience can be awkward and unsettling. Use this skill to see where you land on the spectrum today.

WHAT YOU WILL LEARN

* The connection between listening and silence

* Forms of silence

* The various purposes of silence

* How to practice sitting in silence

* How silence makes you feel

WHAT YOU WILL NEED

* 30 minutes

* A quiet space without distractions

* Somewhere to sit comfortably (yoga mat with pillow, bed, chair, or couch)

* Pen

* Optional: Aromatherapy (candle, essential oil diffuser, room or linen spray)

* Optional: Cell phone or computer to play nature sounds (waves, stream, birds, etc.)

INSTRUCTIONS

1. Prepare your space for reflection by finding a quiet, comfortable place to sit. Use aromatherapy to set the mood and play some nature sounds if you wish.

2. Relax your body and sit there for a few minutes. What do you hear? Smell? Feel? Sit and soak in the space you've prepared, the experience. Sit as long as you want to.

3. When you're ready, take your pen and respond to the following questions:

    *   How do you feel right now? Are you comfortable with this silence? Write down your feelings.

        ----

    *   What are you experiencing?

        ----

    *   What thoughts have come to mind as you sit here?

        ----

    *   Have you had any revelations as you sit here?

        ----

4. Wrap up your silent reflection by taking a few moments to relax and breathe.

    If your thoughts feel hopeless, alarming, or overwhelming, see the resources section (page 146) for links to help in this area.

SKILL 15

Adjusting Rigid Boundaries

There are healthy boundaries, and there are rigid boundaries. Ghosting, or cutting someone off without explanation or opportunity for a dialogue, is one example of the latter. This class of boundary is put in place because people are hurting, healing, or fed up. Maybe they've been "doormats" or are recovering from people-pleasing and don't know how to enforce healthy boundaries. Some individuals still carry the pain of whatever led them to put up these impermeable, zero-tolerance walls. So it makes sense. Although certain situations warrant cutting someone off, rigid boundaries can become unhealthy excuses to keep people away and avoid conflict.

WHAT YOU WILL LEARN

* Why ghosting is the antithesis of listening

* Why rigid boundaries are created

* How to loosen a rigid boundary

* How to apologize

WHAT YOU WILL NEED

* 30 to 45 minutes

* Pen or pencil

INSTRUCTIONS

1. Reflect on your relationships. Ask yourself the following questions:

   a. Why is this boundary in place?

   b. Have I established a boundary I'm realizing is too harsh, or am I willing to reconsider a boundary I set to protect myself?

   c. Would I like to adjust this rigid boundary?

   d. How can I adjust this boundary?

   e. What, if anything, is preventing me from adjusting this boundary?

f. Does taking accountability followed by an apology seem like the next step?

Write about your thoughts.

----

2. If you believe an apology is the next step, read through the following step-by-step approach to apologizing and clearing the air. If fear of rejection or conflict is preventing you from adjusting this boundary, I'd like to walk you through the steps anyway. Then you can decide for yourself.

    a. Reflect on your actions. Take a step back and consider the role you played.

    b. Think about what caused you to respond this way and how you could have handled the issue more effectively.

    c. Take responsibility by admitting your part and say, "I'm sorry" or "I apologize." Avoid the use of *but*, which minimizes the apology (such as "I'm sorry, but I think we were both at fault"). It can also be helpful to explain how you felt at the time, so the other person understands your perspective. Use "I" statements that reserve blame (such as "I felt hurt when you didn't invite me to join you").

    d. Be open to listening by accepting feedback from the other person without interruption. Try not to think about your next response, and use your nonverbal cues to let them know you're listening empathetically.

3. Brainstorm some ways you could use healthy boundaries to address a similar issue in the future.

Rigid Boundaries in Response to Abuse

Sometimes rigid boundaries are necessary, particularly when situations are abusive. Flexible boundaries in these circumstances can be dangerous. These are considered extreme circumstances and do not apply to the purpose of the Adjusting Rigid Boundaries (page 53) activity. Maladaptive uses of power and control, such as intimidation, emotional abuse, isolation, minimizing, denying, blaming, using children, economic abuse, male privilege, coercion and threats, or physical or sexual violence, have no place in healthy relationships. Please seek help by calling the U.S. National Domestic Violence Hotline at 800-799-7233.

CHAPTER 4

Empathy

We all desire to be understood. Empathy, commonly described as the ability to put ourselves in someone else's shoes, is a core component of effective and healthy communication. Without empathy, breakdowns in communication occur. Often, relationships end because empathy isn't used as frequently as needed. Conversely, having empathy as a personal characteristic enables us to better understand others and create a validating experience for them. Follow me as we explore the concept of empathy and how it can be used.

Avoiding Empathetic Failure

According to the *APA Dictionary of Psychology*, empathetic failure is "a lack of understanding of another person's feelings, perceptions, and thoughts." Receiving empathy is vital to our psychological well-being, and having empathy is critical for building healthy relationships—and boundaries. For the sake of this chapter, experiencing empathy signifies feeling known by and connected to another, making an empathetic failure an interruption in connection. Let's explore how this disconnect shows up and what we can do to prevent it from happening.

WHAT YOU WILL LEARN

* What empathetic failure is

* The value of empathy in human development and relationships

* How empathetic failure feels

* How you can show empathy (through self-reflection)

WHAT YOU WILL NEED

* 15 to 20 minutes

* Pen

INSTRUCTIONS

1. Recall a time when you felt misunderstood, minimized, or invalidated. Journal about that experience. How did it make you feel? How could it have been prevented through empathy?

----

2. Now think of a time that you might have failed to use empathy with another person. Journal your thoughts. How did you react? How could you have responded more empathetically?

------

3. Finally, reflect or write about some ways you can show empathy to another whose values might not align with yours. Consider ways you can honor their feelings without compromising your own.

It's important to acknowledge that you can respect the differences in someone else while also maintaining your core values. Understanding does not mean you have to make someone else's priorities yours. Recovering people pleasers, this message is for you! As you progress in building healthier boundaries, remember that if you fall into old habits, it's OK as long as you aren't paralyzed by them. This kind of transformation requires practice, so check in with yourself regularly to ensure you're being authentic.

Guarding Empathy

Being an empathetic person comes with many wonderful attributes from which you and others benefit. However, there are drawbacks—especially for those who are already naturally sensitive or in tune with others and the world in a spiritually intuitive way—such as depleting yourself in the interest of others' needs. Let's gauge your empathic experience and explore some useful self-care practices you can apply whenever needed.

WHAT YOU WILL LEARN

* Whether you are prone to empathy fatigue

* Signs of empathy fatigue

* The value of *no* in response to empathy fatigue

* Practical self-care ideas (through self-reflection)

WHAT YOU WILL NEED

* 15 to 20 minutes

* Pen

INSTRUCTIONS

1. Check off any of the scenarios you have experienced:

    Attended a nonessential event that I didn't really want to go to.

    Helped another person out of obligation though it was inconvenient.

    Didn't ask for help because I didn't want to inconvenience anyone.

    Let someone ahead of me in line even though I was in a rush.

    Missed an opportunity because I didn't want to impose on someone.

    Listened to someone's long story over the phone when I really wanted to hang up.

- Honored someone's regular taxing requests.

- Listened to the same story over and over.

- Acquiesced to a person's insistence that I do what they want even when I really wanted to do something else.

2. If you can relate to some of these scenarios, you're probably pretty familiar with empathy fatigue. In her book *The Sugar Jar: Create Boundaries, Embrace Self-Healing, and Enjoy the Sweet Things in Life*, mental wellness advocate Yasmine Cheyenne uses a sugar jar metaphor to describe how we may not have the capacity for certain people, places, or situations and the importance of "attending to [the sugar in] our own jars." Empathy fatigue can result if we don't attend to ourselves.

   Avoiding empathy fatigue takes diligence, vigilance even, to protect our mental, emotional, spiritual, and physical energy. Here are some warning signs:

   * Feeling overwhelmed

   * Feeling drained

   * Feeling stressed from taking on the emotions of others

   * Feeling burned out on people

When these signs arise, relief can be as simple as applying one word: *no. No* to the invitation if the thought of attending stresses you out. *No* to allowing others to use your caring nature and keen listening skills as justification to emotionally dump on you. (We'll explore these concepts in greater detail in chapter 5.)

Now that you've recognized some typical drivers and symptoms of empathy fatigue, let's consider how you can respond to your own needs more effectively.

1. Look at each scenario on the checklist. Did any of these really resonate with you? How might you respond next time, in a caring way that still serves your needs?

   _____

   _____

   _____

   _____

2. Think about an obligation or situation you are looking to get out of. What can you say or do to remove yourself from this situation?

   _____

   _____

   _____

   _____

3. Now ask yourself, *What can I do to take care of myself better? What small steps can I take to defend my own time, space, and needs (and keep that sugar jar filled!)?*

   _____

   _____

   _____

   _____

Recognizing Empathy Barriers

Let's talk about judgment, a barrier to empathy. When we make judgments, the analytic mind leads, instead of the heart and senses. Empathy wants to join with the person sharing, while judgment seeks to dissect the details. To shift toward a more empathetic viewpoint, the goal is to release judgment and be present with what the other person needs—not what you think is best for them. This tool isn't about changing who you are. It's about identifying your tendencies so you can take steps toward shifting your perspective if needed.

WHAT YOU WILL LEARN

* How judgment can hinder empathy

* Your habits as a listener

* How you tend to react to the concept of empathy

* How shifting your perspective might affect your empathy

WHAT YOU WILL NEED

* 15 minutes

* Pen

INSTRUCTIONS

1. Read and reflect on the following quotes:

   "Empathy [has] no script. There is no right way or wrong way to do it. It's simply listening, holding space, withholding judgment, emotionally connecting, and communicating that incredibly healing message of 'You're not alone.'"

   —BRENÉ BROWN, SCHOLAR

"Too often we underestimate the power of a touch, a smile, a kind word, a listening ear, an honest compliment, or the smallest act of caring, all of which have the potential to turn a life around."

—LEO BUSCAGLIA, AUTHOR

2. What are your thoughts on these sentiments? What parts do you agree or disagree with? What barriers, if any, came up as you read? Any judgments?

    ----

3. Think of a recent time when somebody sought your empathy. What were your feelings? How did you respond? Do these quotes shift your perspective, and if so, how?

Self-Compassion

When you are kind to yourself, you're better able to care for others. You're more likely to come into relationships with empathy and understanding that we are all flawed and deserve love. Conversely, if you have a harsh inner critic, or if you internalize judgmental, shame-filled narratives or falsehoods, this isn't serving you well. It's toxic to your well-being. It can make relationships and boundaries complicated. And it can change. If you relate, let's make space for something new. Something restorative. Even if you are compassionate toward yourself, we can all use a good affirmation.

WHAT YOU WILL LEARN

* How self-compassion fosters empathy

* How self-compassion can make you feel

* Which messages you may need to hear

* How to challenge a harsh inner critic

* How practice can help you replace old faulty narratives

WHAT YOU WILL NEED

* 15 minutes

* Quiet space free of distractions

* Aromatherapy (optional)

* Nature sounds (optional)

* Pen

INSTRUCTIONS

1. Sit comfortably, using aromatherapy and soft nature sounds if you wish.

2. Begin with five slow, deep breaths. In through your nose. Out through your mouth.

3. Read the following statements aloud (adding your own if desired):

   * I give myself grace for the things I did not know.

   * I forgive myself for the things I did or didn't do.

   * I am constantly learning and growing.

   * I'm grateful for the lessons that hardships in life have taught me.

   * It's OK that I don't know all the answers.

   * My life has meaning and purpose.

   * I am more than what I've been through.

   * I am resilient.

   * Joy is my strength and my birthright.

   * _____

   * _____

   * _____

   * _____

   * _____

   * _____

4. Reflect. How was this experience for you? Strange? Awkward? Soothing? How did/would you fine-tune it? What would you do differently next time?

   _____

   _____

   _____

   _____

   _____

5. Come back to these affirmations often. Consider posting them where you'll see them.

   If you deal with a harsh inner critic:

   a. Think about the message your inner critic is sending. Write it down in your journal.

   b. "Fact-check" by examining whether that thought is based on a feeling (such as anxiety or fear) or a verifiable fact. Write your findings in your journal.

   c. If the thought is based on a feeling, ask yourself why this is so.

   d. Now defend yourself. For example, if your inner critic berates you for your "lackluster" presentation at work, remind yourself that it's not easy to speak in front of a group and that several colleagues seemed interested and asked questions. Write your defending message in your journal.

   e. If the thought is based on a verifiable fact, give yourself grace. Nobody's perfect. Provide reassurance and talk to yourself as you would a good friend, and consider what you can do moving forward to grow from the experience.

   f. Remember to defend yourself so you can reframe and guide the narratives you tell yourself in a supportive way. We can erase and replace false stories that have framed our lives—faulty thinking that was either passed on to us or we somehow inadvertently internalized along the way. As we grow in confidence, we no longer need to feed into the narrative we've been cloaked in. We can be empowered to believe, do, and be in ways that align with the vision of well-being we see for ourselves.

SKILL 20

Parts of Empathy

Let's look at the three parts of empathy. **Cognitive empathy** is choosing to pro-verbially put oneself in another's shoes (*How would I feel if that happened to me?*). **Emotive empathy** is about how the other person's experience makes you feel (*It makes me feel angry just thinking about what happened*). **Empathic action** is being present and/or acting on the situation (*I will sit with you, in silence if needed,* or *I will donate my time in support of you*). You'll see how they can work together to create the ultimate expression of empathy.

WHAT YOU WILL LEARN

* The three parts of empathy

* How each part of empathy supports the recipient

* Ways to provide various forms of empathy

* How empathy makes you feel

WHAT YOU WILL NEED

* 20 minutes

* Pen

* Markers or colored pencils (optional)

INSTRUCTIONS

1. Think about a time when you experienced any of the three parts of empathy. Fill in the corresponding pictures by writing about those experiences and how it felt to have each kind of support.

2. Feel free to color the pictures as you brainstorm some ways you can offer these kinds of empathy to another person. Set an intention to offer empathy during your day.

COGNITIVE
EMPATHY

EMOTIVE
EMPATHY

EMPATHIC
ACTION

CHAPTER 5

Emotional Boundaries

For the purpose of this chapter, let's define *emotional boundaries* as your emotional limits. Identifying them will aid you in recognizing if and when they're crossed. This chapter will heighten your awareness and understanding when your emotional capacity has been reached. Then, using the assertive communication lessons from chapter 1, you'll explore tools that can help you become more proactive (instead of being reactive or assuming the posture of a helpless bystander) while someone saps your energy—or bulldozes over you.

Feeling for Enough

When is enough *enough* for you? When a conversation becomes more burdensome than you can handle, removing yourself from it might be just what you need. You may bid everyone farewell and physically leave a space. This is a literal form of disengaging. Perhaps you have nothing to contribute to the dialogue, feeling more comfortable as a listener or resisting the call to join a negative discourse. Silence is another way to disengage. It all depends on what you need; that's why being in tune with your needs is so important. Let's process your feelings through this skill so you can "feel for enough" in your future interactions.

WHAT YOU WILL LEARN

* Ways to disengage

* How to advocate for yourself when emotional limits are reached

* When you've had enough

* Sensations experienced when you're emotionally drained or overwhelmed

WHAT YOU WILL NEED

* 15 minutes

* Pen

INSTRUCTIONS

Think about a time when you had a conversation that felt like it sucked the life out of you, and respond to the following:

1. How did you feel **emotionally** during and after that conversation? Overwhelmed? Agitated? Irritable? Angry? Sad? Drained? Exhausted? Anxious? Stressed? Discouraged? Something else?

    _____

    _____

    _____

2. Try recalling how you felt **physically** during or after this conversation: Tired? Tearful? Sweaty? Or what you felt: Stomachache? Muscle tension or spasms? Headache? Lower back pain? Increased heart rate? Something else?

_____

_____

_____

3. Journal a bit about how you might have honored your emotional boundaries in this instance. What could you have done to separate yourself from this uncomfortable situation?

_____

_____

_____

With these insights, you can make informed decisions in establishing or refreshing emotional boundaries. When you realize you were in a fairly decent mood before a conversation or interaction, but afterward, you wished you hadn't answered the phone or checked the email, this is an indication that your emotions and sense of well-being need attention. Make time for yourself. Be curious about why you feel the way you do. Our next tool covers this more.

Self-Care Check-In

Long day? Feeling stressed? All over the place? Relationship struggles? Just experienced a loss? If so, don't be surprised when you're unable to hold space for your BFF, who is struggling with their own issues. We're not superhuman, with an unlimited reservoir of energy or physical and emotional strength. We have to replenish, rest, and allow for renewal—and *often*. When you're already over-whelmed and someone you love wants to extract more from you, here are some practical ways to integrate self-care practices as emotional boundaries.

WHAT YOU WILL LEARN

* What causes you stress

* Specific self-care practices that work for you

* How mindfulness enhances self-care

* How self-care can help you be present for others

WHAT YOU WILL NEED

* 15 minutes

* Internet access (optional)

* Pen

INSTRUCTIONS

1. Using the example provided, think of some situations you've faced or are currently trying to navigate.

    Situation: Long day at work; you're feeling depleted, and going home feels like beginning another shift for your second job.

    Self-care solution: Decompress before going home by taking a walk around the block.

2. Write down a stressful or overwhelming situation that applies to you.

    ----

3. Think about what you need when this situation occurs. Identify a self-care solution that would work for you, being as specific as possible. Feel free to use the ideas provided or use your own. You can also search for terms like *hydrotherapy, horticultural therapy*, and *aromatherapy* to learn more about their benefits and how to use them.

   * Visit a coffee shop
   * Stop at a favorite store
   * Spend time in nature
   * Work out or play a sport
   * Take a mindful walk
   * Engage your senses

   * Go to bed early
   * Unplug
   * Shower or bathe
   * Use aromatherapy
   * Do a guided meditation
   * Listen to something uplifting

4. When you implement your self-care plan, make it as mindful and intentional as possible. For example, if you visit a coffee shop, journal about your day there, read, or just people-watch as you sip. If you go for a walk or spend time in nature, engage your senses: What are you seeing? Smelling? Hearing? Feeling? If you're going to bed, make a relaxing ritual for yourself. Dim the lights, unplug, and retreat early to optimize the process of neurogenesis—the daily birthing of new nerve cells, which enhances mental benefits.

5. Repeat steps 2 through 4 as often as you wish.

   Replenishing ourselves does not require a vacation every other week. I hope this activity normalizes how easy it can be to check in and take care of your needs before assisting others with theirs. Most of us are just one decision away from discovering the solution to any presenting challenge—and it's often as simple as stepping back and taking a little time to tend to our own needs.

SKILL 23

Where to Share

Some people share too much too soon. Being less chatty can fine-tune your observation of people and your listening skills—important tools for healthy relationships and knowing what to share and with whom. To this end, gauge whether people's actions are in alignment with their words: Are they consistent? Do they respect your emotional boundaries? Are they dismissive? Do they tell you how to feel instead of validating your experience? Your observations can help you answer these kinds of questions. Even the closest relationships experience occasional communication missteps, and a proactive response can help clear the air and set expectations. Let's establish some emotional boundaries.

WHAT YOU WILL LEARN

* How listening and observing others helps discern trustworthiness

* How to set emotional boundaries with people

WHAT YOU WILL NEED

* 15 minutes

* Pen

INSTRUCTIONS

Read each scenario and come up with an emotional boundary. The first one is provided for you.

SCENARIO	EMOTIONAL BOUNDARY
A conversation with a friend becomes uncomfortable because of a misunderstanding, and the friend wants to end the conversation instead of working through the awkwardness.	"Please give me a moment. I think what I said was misunderstood. This is actually what I was trying to say, if it's OK to explain. If not, I'd like to share later." (Assertively communicate in a way that respects you and them.)
You're feeling anxious and worried about work. You vent to your partner, and their response is "Just pray about it and it'll be fine."	
You've shared something personal with a supposed confidant, and that information comes up later in a group chat.	
While busy at work, you receive a call from a family member who wants to emotionally vent to you. You don't have time for this.	

Was this easy for you? Were you able to respond clearly and assertively? Do you feel confident that you can use these kinds of responses in real-life situations?

Intuition Fruition

Have you ever ignored gut feelings about a person or situation? The reaction usually goes something like this: "I *knew* I shouldn't have told them" or "I had a feeling this would happen." If we seemingly *know*, why do we override our intuition? Perhaps, somewhere along the way, we lost trust in ourselves. Learning how to trust our intuition takes practice—especially when we've mastered doing the opposite. But we can learn, and when we do, we can make informed decisions that serve us best.

WHAT YOU WILL LEARN

* How to increase trust in yourself

* How to respond to your intuition in a real-life situation

* How intuition and observation can guide boundaries

* Strategies to improve your intuition

WHAT YOU WILL NEED

* 15 minutes, plus time to complete the strategies

* Pen

INSTRUCTIONS

1. Think about a time when your intuition was activated but you ignored your instincts instead of trusting them to guide your decision. What could you do differently in the future? Are there any current situations in which you can practice trusting in yourself and let your intuition guide you? If so, write out what you've felt so far or *know* about the situation intuitively. Does an emotional boundary need to be created? What is it that you need, and how can you meet that need?

    ----

2. Read over the following strategies for improving your intuition. Test them over the next week or so, and see what comes up for you.

    * **Reduce stress.** Stress affects your decision-making abilities, including the ability to discern what your intuition is telling you. Using Boundaries and Self-Care (page 41) is an antidote to stress, as are the following strategies.

    * **Tune into your body.** When your body aches, it's telling you that either you're getting sick or you worked those muscles hard. Likewise, when your gut or brain tells you something's not right, listen—that's valid information, too.

    * **Tune into others.** As you practiced in Where to Share (page 76), observing others and being a good listener provide important information that can help you discern others' character and intentions.

    * **Meditate.** Meditation doesn't have to mean hours of lying still—there are great, purposeful guided meditations online that feel more like short stories you can listen to. Check out YouTube for guided meditations that focus on strengthening your intuition.

    * **Be mindful.** So many of us run on autopilot that we miss most of what's around us—can you relate? By setting the intention to be present in your tasks and encounters throughout the day, you'll enjoy increased awareness, clarity, and decision-making.

    * **Affirm yourself.** Write down an affirmation that reminds you to trust yourself. It can be as simple as "Trust your inner knowing" or "Pay attention to how you feel." Post it somewhere you'll see it.

3. Did any of these tools help? Can you think of other ideas? Write about them here.

SKILL 25

Responding Well

Have you ever misunderstood a situation or comment but didn't realize the misunderstanding until after you overreacted to it? Have you ever jumped the gun, even just a little? Responded with a long text message when the situation didn't warrant it? Was snippy and later realized someone's comment was actually a compliment or harmless joke? Let's look at why some people overreact, and then let's talk about how to prevent overreactions in a few simple steps.

WHAT YOU WILL LEARN

* Reasons people overreact

* The adverse impact of defensiveness on healthy boundaries

* How to prevent overreactions

WHAT YOU WILL NEED

* 5 minutes to read, plus time to self-reflect and/or phone a friend for feedback

* Your core values list from Grounded in Knowing (page 18)

* Pen

INSTRUCTIONS

Before we start, to provide a little perspective, those who tend to overreact usually have a backstory. Being silenced often or not receiving necessary validation as a child can make for defensive or argumentative adults who believe they must force their message to be heard. This is the result of not having those young voices valued. They were expected to "be seen and not heard," rarely considered in decisions that impacted them, or not offered an explanation as to why things happened around them. Those early experiences can create a guarded stance that is always ready to fire and protect. Those defenseless little kids turn into grownups who overcompensate for the helplessness they once experienced. I know this firsthand, and it's processed frequently in therapy with clients. Whether you can relate to this backstory or you just want to avoid jumping the gun, these tips can help.

1. Read the following tips for preventing overreactions:

   * **Consider the source.** Is the person you are potentially about to lose your cool with someone who mistreats you? Dismisses or minimizes your feelings? Emotionally dumps on you or is irritable with you? If the answer is no, consider pausing long enough to give the individual the benefit of the doubt, along with time to clarify the meaning or intention behind what was said. If the answer is yes, try to respond firmly, clearly, and calmly. Later, reflect on your response and consider how creating boundaries might help you deflect future negative encounters.

   * **Revisit your core values.** What's important to you? If you value things like honesty, authentic relationships, or personal growth, ask yourself, *What kind of reaction will I feel good about later? Is this misunderstanding a chance to work through an awkward situation since I value this friendship?*

   * **Honor your worth.** If flying off the handle is a common reaction for you—perhaps one that has resulted in unwanted isolation, unfriending, being blocked, and so on—you're worth the effort it will take to learn how to respond differently. Even though our early experiences may have impacted us, they don't have to continue to shape us. To know better is to choose to do things that help us live out this life in better ways—instead of repeating the same maladaptive habits when we have access to so much more.

2. From what you just read, think on the areas that resonate with you. Journal about what changes, if any, you'd like to make.

   ----

3. The next time you feel tempted to react harshly, pause and consider what you've learned before reacting. Afterward, journal about the experience. Was this information helpful, and if so, how? How did you react? What was the outcome? Was the issue resolved? How did you feel as a result of the exchange and your response?

Boundary Issues (and How to Talk about Them)

Welcome to part 2, where we will explore relatable issues for those of us who struggle with setting healthy boundaries. Each of the five chapters covers a different area in which we can encounter boundary issues: romantic relationships, family, friendship, work, and community.

We'll look at scenarios that describe an issue, then explore solutions using guided therapeutic steps that apply tools from part 1 of this book. The goal is to build the confidence, comfort, and familiarity to integrate these communication skills into your life, creating healthy boundaries within these areas. Are you ready? OK, let's go!

CHAPTER 6

Romantic Relationships

Although exciting and fun and even intoxicating, romantic relationships come with challenges, and here's one reason: We don't always communicate the things we need, want, or value with our partners. We don't always listen. And we may fail to implement healthy boundaries consistently. When these things happen, trouble in paradise can begin to develop. Through brief vignettes, we'll explore five common issues that arise within romantic relationships, explore what's going on from a therapeutic lens, and then address these problems using some of the tools discussed in the first section of this book.

Paying for the Past

Alisha and Mike were close friends and classmates in high school, but they didn't begin dating until later, when Alisha relocated to their hometown. Back in high school, Alisha was quiet and focused on academics. Mike's focus was to date as many girls as possible, but he never pursued Alisha—until now. She was initially shocked by his interest in her and well aware of his high school shenanigans. That knowledge, as well as residual feelings from a painful breakup a year ago, made Alisha reluctant, but eventually she gave a relationship with Mike a try. Six months into their courtship, they've arrived in couples therapy after Mike initiated contact to discuss some trust challenges.

What Is Going On

Mike's high school reputation and the ending of Alisha's last relationship due to her ex's cheating have impeded her ability to be open and build trust with him. During therapy, Mike reiterates why he didn't pursue Alisha in high school: He wasn't ready to be serious with anyone, and he valued their friendship too much to risk starting something he knew he wasn't mature enough to handle at the time. Alisha's challenge is separating the indiscretions of a past relationship from her present-day reality. She sometimes recalls the teenage-playboy version of Mike, who was similar to her unfaithful ex.

Address the Issue

Despite the alignment between Mike's words and actions, Alisha's having difficulty believing Mike's devotion to her. In addition to therapy, Alisha would benefit from practicing Reflective Listening (page 48). She isn't hearing or fully internalizing what Mike tells her. They can practice the skill together to strengthen their communication and her ability to hear and receive Mike's verbal commitment to their relationship.

Here's how reflective listening might work for them:

> MIKE: "Alisha, like I've told you before, I knew there was something special about you in high school, but I wasn't ready for anything serious. You were the friend I could talk to about anything. When you moved back home, I couldn't pass up the opportunity to add to what we'd already had. I don't like being penalized for being a kid then and for what that other dude did to you. I'm not him."

> THERAPIST: "Alisha, what did you hear Mike say?"

> ALISHA: "Mike, you said you didn't try to date me in high school because you knew you weren't ready and I was special. You also said you wanted to build on the friendship we had already established, and it is unfair of me to judge you based on who you were in school and what happened before our relationship. You are not him."

> MIKE: "Yes, that is correct. I love you, girl!"

As Alisha gets stronger and builds her trust, Intuition Fruition (page 78) will also provide Alisha with the ability to trust her gut in addition to trusting Mike. This can help cement her resolve in knowing that Mike really is devoted to her. And she can use the tools of empathy (chapter 4) to reassure him that she's devoted, too!

Discussion Notes

We all have a past. Let's not allow it to distort the reality that is before us now. Alisha can experience the love of her life if she actively seeks healing from her previous relationship and allows herself to fully absorb the love Mike gives as the man he is today by listening closely and acknowledging how his words and actions align.

Boundaries with Exes

Dara and Harper, both in their 40s, have been married for seven years and are parents to five-year-old twins. Dara works from home, while Harper, an entrepreneur, has just acquired a new contract that demands more overtime and later nights than usual. This contract also comes with regular contact with Harper's ex-fiancée, Mia, who works in the same industry and won a different bid for the same 90-day project. Mia often jokes that Harper is "the one that got away," and now that they're working closely for the next three months, Mia has begun to test Harper's boundaries by becoming increasingly flirtatious.

What Is Going On

Mia's lack of successful relationships since she called off her engagement to Harper 10 years ago has left her regretting that decision. At the time, her focus was building her empire as an entrepreneur. Her regrets are not Harper's to carry, but maintaining respectful interactions with Mia is apparently his responsibility. Dara is aware the two have been working together and trusts her spouse. Harper has attempted to ward off Mia with avoidance and passive responses to her blatant flirting, but Mia keeps persisting.

Address the Issue

There are a few issues within this scenario, the first being Harper's passivity with Mia's advances and the discomfort it has created for him. Harper needs to practice Passing on Passivity (page 26) and Assertively Advocating (page 23). With a strong sense of his core values intact (Grounded in Knowing, page 18), there is no desire to pursue anything but the completion of this project with Mia so the contractual obligations can be met and the final check deposited into his bank account.

Harper wants to spare Mia's feelings, which is why he has been unable to successfully establish firmer boundaries with her. If I were working with Harper, I'd encourage him to view boundary setting as a self-care strategy (Boundaries and

Self-Care, page 41). His discomfort with Mia's nonprofessional communication toward him is an indication something needs to be addressed.

Let's take a look at practicing communicating assertively from Harper's perspective:

1. THINK ABOUT IT: What's the problem? *Mia's unwelcomed flirting. I no longer want to prioritize her feelings over my comfort.*

2. GET TO THE POINT: "Mia, I feel uncomfortable when you flirt. I haven't thought of you in that way in years, and my only focus is to get this job completed. Our work together is strictly professional. I'm sure we can make this work. Can you?"

3. MIND YOUR NONVERBALS: *I used consistent eye contact and relaxed body language, and I did not smile or smirk.*

4. CHECK YOUR TONE: *I spoke in a regular tone, without elevating my voice.*

Discussion Notes

If you're dealing with an ex who doesn't respect your present circumstances, it's your responsibility to protect yourself and your current relationship regardless of how the other person chooses to behave. Have assertive conversations as needed, and be mindful not to prioritize someone else's needs or wants over your values.

ISSUE 3

Losing Autonomy

Laura Charles's friends have noticed changes in "LC" ever since she began dating Bruce about a month ago. LC, a longtime vegan, has started eating meat and doesn't seem to have time for her close friends anymore. She's also stopped engaging in creative activities, like painting, cross-stitching, and ceramic making. She has instead begun golfing with Bruce, who loves the sport, and joins him whenever possible, even though she has expressed that she finds it boring. She seems like a different person, which has her friends baffled and wondering what's going on.

What Is Going On

It isn't uncommon to change or "lose yourself" during a romantic relationship, especially in the beginning. Love is intoxicating! But this submersion into new love and all its trappings can result in compromise, including compromising parts of who you are and even your values. You may begin disregarding your standards or pursuits for the sake of the relationship. LC has experienced stomach cramps because of her dietary choices, and she's forfeited opportunities to engage in hobbies she loves and to spend time with those she cares for—all evidence of a struggle to maintain authenticity and individuality in a new relationship.

Address the Issue

This lighthearted scenario is a mild example of how losing autonomy can happen in a relationship. LC would say she really knows herself (Grounded in Knowing, page 18), but her core values of spontaneity and connection have begun to impede upon her equal need for independence and balance within this new relationship. Although she enjoys spending time with Bruce, even on the green, she isn't expressing that she'd also like to do ceramics, is experiencing digestion issues, and misses connecting with her friends.

This issue can be addressed by reminding LC who she is and empowering her to maintain authenticity as her budding relationship develops. She can use

Connecting Strengths and Values (page 32) to help her explore the importance of self-awareness (you'll see how this skill can also help her reconnect with her friends). LC can have an honest and assertive conversation with Bruce, sharing her thoughts and interests and desire to continue pursuing them. She can also practice creating and communicating healthier boundaries with her time, hobbies, and diet by enlisting Boundaries and Self-Care (page 41).

For example, she can work on one of her cross-stitch projects as Bruce golfs if she decides to tag along but not play. She can also begin to take initiative in selecting what eateries they patronize and introduce Bruce to some of the vegan dishes she enjoys. Through communication and compromise, they can see if they are truly, authentically compatible.

Discussion Notes

Opposites do attract. Whether that difference be in temperament or the things we like to do for fun, we're all unique, and that's OK. Differences are problematic only when they don't support healthy values, compromise, and our individual sense of self.

ISSUE 4

Money Matters

Brenda is becoming increasingly frustrated with Sonny's spending habits. When he was laid off his job, she suggested they move in together. They thought it would help Sonny hold on to some of his savings while he searched for employment. The couple agreed to share all household expenses, and Sonny is adhering to the agreement. However, as a self-professed sneakerhead, Sonny buys shoes to cope, and he's buying them pretty often. Brenda is frustrated with Sonny's use of retail therapy as a coping strategy and feels that it's irresponsible to keep spending without employment. She's telling him what she thinks of his frivolous purchases.

What Is Going On

Navigating finances is a hot topic in couples therapy. Contention arises due to differences in budgeting styles as well as variations in spending habits and money mindsets. Beneath Brenda's frustration is fear that Sonny's habit combined with his commitment to contribute financially will deplete his savings, which counters the original goal of moving in together. Little does Brenda know, Sonny's savings are healthy. He manages his finances and does not spend on much else outside the household expenses. Likewise, little does Sonny realize, the source of Brenda's anxiety surrounding finances is rooted in the instability she experienced growing up.

Address the Issue

Let's look at the facts: For Sonny, buying new shoes helps him feel better, and he has budgeted for every purchase made. He communicates this with Brenda each time. She is allowing her fear to replace empathy toward Sonny during this emotionally low transitional space he's in. She was traumatized by her family's struggles, and now financial matters terrify her. She counters her fear by being very rigid with her money and now, apparently, with Sonny's as well.

They've never lived together before, and this is their first time sharing financial responsibilities.

Brenda would benefit from Recognizing Empathy Barriers (page 63). She would realize that her past experience leads her to be overly critical of Sonny's shoe buying and impacts her ability to express empathy. She can also use a Self-Care Check-In (page 74) to create a wellness plan that can assist her with managing her anxiety.

It's also time to share (Where to Share, page 76). Her intuition tells her so. Regardless of the sneaker collecting, Brenda finds Sonny to be an attentive, caring person who contributes in so many ways. He is trustworthy enough to hear her story. Once he does, he'll better understand, and, hopefully, he will share a bit himself, alleviating Brenda's concern about his financial state. Once she hears this, she's likely to enlist the art of apology (Adjusting Rigid Boundaries, page 53) for adding unnecessary stress to Sonny during a difficult time in his life.

Finally, Empathetic Listening (page 46) can only help this new live-in couple. Brenda can support Sonny as he works through his feelings of being laid off, and Sonny can listen empathetically as Brenda works through some of her uncomfortable narratives around money. Maybe Brenda will even be inspired to clear out a closet for Sonny's shoes.

Discussion Notes

Cohabiting can expose a lot about people. Although money is the topic explored within this section, the theme can be anything. We all have unresolved matters— the goal is not to project them onto others. Of course, one has to be aware this is happening, and a good therapist can help unpack this further.

Kids, or Not?

College sweethearts Ron and Vanessa have been planning out their lives together since they began dating: everything from what kind of home they want, where to live, and thoughts on children. Vanessa is the eldest of four siblings, and Ron is an only child. Every holiday season, Ron looks forward to spending time with Vanessa's big family. He imagines re-creating those same types of memories with a family of their own one day. Ron loves listening to Vanessa's childhood stories and admires the bond she has with her siblings. However, Vanessa has expressed she doesn't want children. Ron is struggling to accept this.

What Is Going On

Ron adores Vanessa and has wanted to become a father most of his life. Even though Vanessa has been adamant from the start regarding not wanting children, he thought he could persuade her. He can't imagine starting a family with anyone else but the love of his life. Ron was raised in a single-parent home by his devoted father. He attributes so much of his successes to his father's very active presence in his life. He wants to be that kind of dad one day. With a different lived experience as the eldest, Vanessa feels like she has partially raised kids—her siblings—already.

Address the Issue

When Vanessa shared early on in their relationship that she didn't want kids, Ron had an opportunity to hear her words as they were. He chose to filter her wishes through his desires and dismissed her, thinking she'd change her mind. Whether you're rooting for Ron or Vanessa, this is a complicated situation.

Parts of Empathy (page 68) is a tool this couple can practice both individually and together, using the knowledge they have of each other's background and family history. Let's apply the three parts to their situation:

COGNITIVE EMPATHY

* Ron, how would you feel if you missed out on aspects of your childhood because you were a caregiver to your younger siblings?

* Vanessa, can you imagine coming from a small family and being the only child in the home?

EMOTIVE EMPATHY

* Ron, can you understand why Vanessa feels overwhelmed by the thought of becoming a parent?

* Vanessa, can you imagine how lonely Ron's experience could have been and why Ron wants the opportunity to raise his own children? Can you see why he hopes to be the father his dad was to him?

EMPATHIC ACTION

* Take turns sitting with the other and being present in the new awareness of the other person's perspective. Ron and Vanessa can then discuss their experience with this awareness.

Ron and Vanessa have some work ahead of them. They can enlist many of the tools in this book to help them establish what's most important to them (Grounded in Knowing, page 18), understand how the other is feeling (Empathetic Listening, page 46), reflect on any barriers to empathy (Recognizing Empathy Barriers, page 63), and even consider whether they are prepared to reconsider their boundaries on this issue (Adjusting Rigid Boundaries, page 53).

Discussion Notes

The decision to become a parent is huge. When people think they can change the other person's mind about children (or anything), they may find themselves in a predicament when it doesn't happen. Empathy can help Ron and Vanessa see the other side; however, it may not be enough to convince either party to change.

CHAPTER 7

Family

As a trained marriage and family therapist, I hold the topic of family near and dear to my heart. It is also the only topic that has come up in some capacity in just about every single session I've had with clients since my start as an intern decades ago. Navigating through familial issues is a complicated matter, so applying healthy communication skills and boundaries is a must!

Family Too-Togetherness

Claudette is excited to host her six adult children for the holidays. Most of them live out of state. Having them home, all together again, is something she looks forward to every year. Her excitement shifts into feeling overwhelmed as she considers all the preparatory tasks and errands ahead. Not to mention the petty arguments that arise over lack of space, unresolved issues, and sibling rivalries. She knows she's going to be exhausted when this is all over. *Why can't it be easier?* she asks herself.

What Is Going On

Claudette has never been great at knowing her limits or setting boundaries with herself and her children. She doesn't know how to assertively ask for help when she needs it, and when she's fed up, she uses a manipulative tone her kids have mastered ignoring since their youth. She's also under the impression that because she's the host, she must do it all despite being physically drained. She cleans, prepares meals, and gets ready for her guests. By the time they all arrive, she's suffering from back pain and muscle spasms and has to greet them from her recliner.

Address the Issue

For Claudette to get the support she needs, she'll have to assess what changes she's willing to make. All the children know how to cook and can assist with preparing dishes, but they've been under the impression that Ma Dear, as they call her, enjoys cooking everything because she's previously declined their offers to help. Additionally, her children's families have expanded, and everyone wants to stay at the house. She's inflating air mattresses and squeezing them everywhere. How can she mitigate all of this?

By Assertively Advocating (page 23), doing a Self-Care Check-In (page 74), and respecting her own limits by Feeling for Enough (page 72), Claudette can set some healthier holiday boundaries and express her needs. It may be a challenge, since Claudette's always had a certain way of doing things and communicating. Claudette's children can also employ some empathy, recognizing that their mom is getting older and their group is getting bigger. Wake up, kids, and help Ma Dear!

Now for the tricky part: What are some ways she can deal with family conflict if and when it arises? Should she disengage? Or should she set the ground rules before they arrive? Good news: Claudette has done her homework here. She's already talked with her children about not getting involved in any disputes. They're adults, and the expectation is to settle conflicts among themselves.

Discussion Notes

When you know you'll be spending a lot of time with family, plan ahead. Set boundaries with gift giving, emotional investments, participation, and potential areas of conflict. Pay attention to your needs and advocate for them. Check in with how you feel, and prepare for self-care solutions—one of the best of which can be a cheerful departing farewell: "Thanks for a great time! Gotta go, see you soon!"

Severed Siblings

Teri is five years older than her sister, Maxine. Their parents divorced when Maxine was a baby; however, Teri was old enough to witness her mom's crying spells and bouts of sadness. Young Teri often consoled her mom and wondered why her father had to leave. All the six-year-old knew was that everything was fine before *this new baby arrived*. Fast-forward to adulthood: The sisters haven't spoken in two years, since Maxine became so inebriated that she embarrassed Teri and ruined her 30th birthday celebration. In therapy, Maxine talks about the closer relationship she desires to have with her sister.

What Is Going On

Children often aren't privy to the inner workings of the relationships of their adult caregivers, nor should they be. Unfortunately, sometimes a lack of information can leave children drawing their own conclusions. Teri's six-year-old mind secretly blamed Maxine for their dad leaving and mom crying. Before Maxine, she had a mother, a father, and a happy home. As they grew up, Teri was resentful that her baby sister had to tag along wherever she went. Although Teri put up with a lot from Maxine, the debacle at her party ruptured their relationship.

Address the Issue

Maxine, long identified as a troubled child, also internalized and assumed responsibility for the dissolution of her parents' marriage, though she has no recollection of living in the same home as her father. This reality saddens her. Teri has memories of a loving father and seemingly happy mother in the home, but all Maxine knew was the angry, stressed-out mom.

Maxine has admitted to her therapist that trying an edible for the first time while already tipsy at her sister's party wasn't the best choice, and she's regretted it since. She has been working through Self-Compassion (page 65) with her therapist in preparation to reach out to Teri. Her therapist has instructed her to practice these affirmations at home. She's using them to give herself grace for her past mistakes and the courage to speak to Teri.

Teri has ghosted her sister, so Maxine is uncertain if she will even get the chance to speak with her. On the chance that she does, Maxine's therapist has also asked her to practice what she wants to say to Teri and suggested she use Empathetic Listening (page 46) and Reflective Listening (page 48) as a guideline. Maxine is preparing herself for any feedback Teri may provide. Maxine just wants a chance for a dialogue and, hopefully, to apologize (Adjusting Rigid Boundaries, page 53).

Discussion Notes

So much of what we experience within our families shapes how we view and engage the world and how we see ourselves. No family is perfect, but they are a part of us. The choices our caregivers made are not ours to carry. May you find release from any burden related to this topic. How can you practice self-compassion in this moment?

Faulty Narratives

Maxine and Teri's mother, Maggie, did the best she could after their father aban-doned them. Maggie didn't see it coming; she thought they were happy. It wasn't even a full year after having Maxine when she was served divorce papers at her part-time job. Teri was in second grade; Maxine, in daycare. Maggie's world flipped upside down. She was devastated and frantic—she had to make some major adjustments to support herself and her girls, and fast. This experience left her anxious and depressed, both often manifesting as anger, specifically toward Maxine, who, even as a baby, looked just like her father.

What Is Going On

Transitioning from working part-time to juggling multiple jobs to provide for her family created an immense amount of stress for Maggie. She could no longer afford their home and was forced to move the family into a small apartment. Every time she looked at Maxine, she was reminded of the girls' father's betrayal. As hardships began to snowball, her mode of survival impeded her ability to be a nurturing and empathic mother. She decided her daughters would be tough and independent so they'd never find themselves feeling like she did: desperate and vulnerable. But instead, Teri became angry, and Maxine, rebellious.

Address the Issue

Maggie's anger toward her ex was inadvertently transferred to Maxine, creating a "mother wound." Similar to "daddy issues," a mother wound is a deep pain a child carries within due to emotional pain brought on by a mother or maternal figure.

Maxine logically knows her mother loved her. Maggie worked and provided for her daughters; all basic physical needs were met, but it didn't always feel that way. Maxine didn't feel wanted. She wasn't told how special and loved she was. It seemed that the only way to get mom's attention or a positive emotional response was through academic achievement. Despite her good grades, she got into trouble at school and was often told things like "For being so smart, you sure make some dumb decisions."

Maxine has been in therapy for the last year and a half. She's had a lot to work through, including abandonment issues related to her father, faulty narratives instilled by her mother, her hopes of reconciliation with her sister, necessary behavior modifications, and coping strategies she can use instead of self-medicating.

This has been an arduous journey for her, but she finally realizes she's worth the time, effort, and investment. By establishing her core values (Grounded in Knowing, page 18) and Cultivating Confidence (page 20) along with all the tools referenced in the previous scenario ("Severed Siblings," page 100), Maxine is slowly healing and developing a healthier sense of self.

Discussion Notes

When we are in pain, we can injure others. These injuries aren't always malicious. Whether Maxine chooses to have a conversation with her mother or not, she is on a path to healing as she learns how to make decisions aligned with the version of herself that she desires to be. Her healing is contingent not on her mother changing but on changing herself.

Blended Family Challenges

Charles and Kim are engaged to be married and recently purchased a home. Kim's son is living with them full-time, and they agreed that Charles's daughter, Loren, should have her own room when she stays with them every other weekend. Kim and Loren get along great; in fact, Loren has shared her desire to live there permanently. The wedding is four months away, and Loren is a junior bridesmaid, but her mother—Charles's ex, Meagan—hasn't taken her to get fitted for her dress despite initially promising to do so. Concerned, Kim takes Loren to be fitted, which angers Meagan.

What Is Going On

Separation, marriage, remarriage, or any new romantic partnership can be challenging to navigate when either partner has children from the previous relationship. With effective communication, clear expectations, and healthy boundaries by both parties, co-parenting with an ex can be successful. When interactions aren't pleasant, this dynamic can become uncomfortably complicated for all involved, especially the children. In this case, Loren expressed her desire to live with her dad and Kim full-time, and Loren's mother lashed out. Now she is attempting to sabotage by not taking Loren to get fitted for her dress.

Address the Issue

It isn't uncommon for children to want to live with a noncustodial parent. They may romanticize the idea of what life would be like to live with the other parent if they haven't had the opportunity to do so. Sometimes the nonprimary parent is less of a disciplinarian, which is more attractive to kids as they believe they'll have more fun or an easier time. Those short visits conceal how a full-time experience would actually look. Another reason is the fear of missing out—especially if other children live in the home with the noncustodial parent, they may feel "replaced."

Meagan feels hurt, betrayed, and frightened by the thought of living alone without her daughter and the fact that Loren is seemingly choosing another

woman to live with instead of her own mother. She's always had primary cus-
tody, and she got along fine with Kim up until now—now she feels manipulated.
It's hard for her to empathize with her daughter when her own emotions are this
intense. She's so upset, she can't see straight. But she can make things better.

First, Meagan can circle back to her core values (Grounded in Knowing,
page 18) and strengths (Connecting Strengths and Values, page 32) and remind
herself what's important to her (her child!) and what strengths she has (loyalty
and determination). She can lock into these qualities and decide that even though
her daughter's current wishes are hurtful, they are not going to damage their
relationship. Loren feels the way she feels, and dismissing those feelings will only
make things more difficult.

There's opportunity to deepen the mother-daughter connection if Meagan
empathizes with her daughter (Empathetic Listening, page 46) and seeks to learn
why Loren feels this way. She sits down with Loren and uses Reflective Listening (page 48) to really understand where Loren's coming from. When she realizes
that Loren's desire to live with her father is all about feeling torn and not wanting to miss out, Meagan's heart aches for her daughter. This isn't at all what she
thought. Loren just wants to keep her relationship with her father alive. Meagan
gives her daughter a big hug and promises to call and get Loren some extra time
with her dad and his new partner.

Discussion Notes

It's hard not to take such things personally. Imagine how you would feel if you
were Loren's mom. The most important gift any parent can give their child in the
wake of a broken partnership is emotional stability, achieved through expressions
of love, empathy, and respect for their relationship with the other partner.

Attention-Seeking Auntie

Julian is deep in focus at work when he looks down at his phone and notices five missed phone calls from his aunt Debbie, who didn't leave a message. Thinking perhaps it is an emergency, Julian stops what he's doing and steps outside to return her call. When she picks up, she proceeds to ask Julian for his brother's phone number and then starts complaining about Julian's cousin, who lives with her. *There was no emergency*, Julian realizes. He explains that he thought it was an emergency based on the number of times she called. His aunt laughs and says, "Thank you for the number, baby," then hangs up.

What Is Going On

It's our responsibility to protect our boundaries even though others may not understand or respect them. Sure, receiving phone calls from family members while you're working can be tricky because you're unsure if there is a real need. In this case, Julian's aunt calls him often with these kinds of questions. And Julian usually picks up anyway out of respect and obligation. He sometimes struggles with putting the needs of others before his. He realizes this and thinks he should do something about it, since it frustrates and stresses him out to be interrupted when he's focusing on work.

Address the Issue

Julian is caring and dutiful. He spends a lot of time worrying about others. He often feels like he needs to renew his own energy but doesn't do anything about it. This man needs a Self-Care Check-In (page 74) and a solid self-care plan (Boundaries and Self-Care, page 41) to help him manage daily stressors and schedule time for renewal and enjoyment.

Next, he can specifically address the demands from others, including his aunt. Intuition Fruition (page 78) can help him listen to his gut when it says things like "Call her back later—it's not anything important." Aunt Debbie has done this to him before—and not only to him. Once he acknowledges the pattern, it will help him avoid this disruption to his day. If he feels like he needs to, he can shoot her a quick "Are you OK" or "Call you after work" text. If he's consistent with his boundaries, his aunt will eventually realize that her outreach during work hours doesn't get results. When his aunt manages to slip in with a work interruption, Feeling for Enough (page 72) will help him determine how to respond. With these boundary tools, Julian will be able to reclaim his work time as his own.

Discussion Notes

Communication boundaries are an integral form of self-care. They let us control how we spend our time and keep stressors at bay. It's up to us to communicate our boundaries. Even a nonresponse is communication. It says, *I'm not available*. And that's OK.

CHAPTER 8

Friendships

We aren't intended to journey alone in life, and healthy friendships enhance the voyage we're all on. Ideally, they provide us with a sense of belonging as well as safe, nonjudgment spaces where we can simply be ourselves. That's why it's important to identify and address when those we count as friends aren't making us feel our best. We're not always going to see things the same way as our friends—even our best friends—and this can result in conflict. However, most friendships are worth the effort of working through any conflict that arises.

The Misguided "Helper"

Brandy and Myles have been inseparable since statistics class freshman year. Now seniors at their HBCU, the pair have remained the best of friends and even share the same major. Myles, recently diagnosed with COVID, is quarantined in his apartment and has not attended classes for several days. Their schedules are nearly identical this semester, and in an attempt to be helpful, Brandy decides to request Myles's assignments from his professors. While doing so, she discloses Myles's diagnosis to them without his permission. Myles later receives a text from a random classmate who overheard Brandy.

What Is Going On

This is Myles's first time contracting COVID, and his symptoms have been debilitating. It's a scary experience for him, and his focus is on recovering and resting, not schoolwork. He already regretted attending the concert where he contracted the virus—he didn't even want to go in the first place. He allowed Brandy to talk him into it and came home with COVID; she did not. Now she's picking up assignments he didn't ask for and isn't well enough to work on—plus sharing his health information with others without permission.

Address the Issue

Although Brandy had no malicious intent, she missed the mark by not checking in with her friend before making executive decisions on his behalf. From her perspective, she's had several mild bouts with COVID and thought Myles could stay on track in classes while in quarantine like she's done. Some Reflective Listening (page 48) could help all the Brandys out there. She meant well, but she forgot to check in with Myles to verify if it was actually helpful to *him*. To further hone this skill, Avoiding Empathetic Failure (page 58) will allow for reflection on areas where empathy may be needed.

As for Myles, several tools could have protected him from the situation he found himself in. A Self-Care Check-In (page 74) would have prevented him from going to the concert in the first place once he reflected that he didn't want to attend. He could have used Passing on Passivity (page 26) to construct an effective response declining the invitation. If attending was a matter of not wanting to let his friend down, Myles might consider Guarding Empathy (page 60). Even simpler would be Assertively Advocating (page 23) and enlisting the acceptable one-word boundary—"No."

Discussion Notes

Not everything we deem helpful to us is helpful to another. Check in with those you want to assist, and ask them what they need. Then listen and do that. Brandy is a great friend, and their relationship isn't over. She was just a little thoughtless of Myles's privacy and jumped ahead of what he *needed* from her—more tea and cough drops!

Contrast in Priorities

Zeke texts Dominic at 9 a.m. to confirm the pickup time for their 30th high school reunion that evening. Zeke wants to be on time to the event since he is receiving an alumni award, so he had volunteered to pick Dominic up on the way. Zeke pulls up to Dominic's five minutes early only to discover he isn't even home. When Zeke calls, Dominic doesn't answer. Several minutes later, Dominic calls back and apologetically states he'd lost track of time completing a report that he didn't want to have to bring home and work on over the weekend.

What Is Going On

These two friends have different priorities for the day. Zeke's goal is to arrive by check-in time at the reunion, whereas Dominic's is to avoid bringing work home. Here's the thing: It's OK that their priorities differ. Both goals are equally important, even though each of their goals is different, which is common within any relational dynamic.

Address the Issue

Dominic could have set an alarm to remind him of his plan with Zeke. That way, if he simply got carried away with work, he would have been able to communicate as his day progressed that he was running late or was electing not to ride with Zeke as soon as he realized the report might require him to stay longer at work. Then Zeke could have made adjustments and avoided driving to his home unnecessarily. Dominic could use some help Avoiding Empathetic Failure (page 58).

Zeke could have planned accordingly by not overextending himself or volunteering to pick his friend up for a time-sensitive activity. Dominic didn't ask for a ride; Zeke offered. Guarding Empathy (page 60) could prove valuable in the future in helping Zeke learn how to protect his own needs over his sense of duty to others.

Discussion Notes

It's OK to make decisions based on your needs. Advocating for your own priorities does not mean you're selfish. It simply means you are unwilling to sacrifice yourself or the things you value. The more authentic we are in tending to our needs, whether that is not taking work home or making sure to show up to an event on time, the more those needs are met.

"Nothing-to-Hide" Steven

Steven has a difficult time keeping confidential information to himself and has been accused of oversharing by friends. Steven is a self-described "open book" who has no qualms about airing the details of all aspects of his life to anyone with a listening ear. Secret keeping is not an area of mastery, nor has it ever been a priority for him. "Nothing-to-hide" Steven is disappointed to learn he is the last to find out about an emotionally painful situation one of his close friends, Elle, is facing.

What Is Going On

Elle loves Steven, and although she considers him a friend, she's cautious about what she shares with him. Early in their friendship, she noticed that Steven would share the details of other people's lives with her. She told him she felt uncomfortable with this. Steven made some changes but still slipped up from time to time, so when faced with her own personal challenges, Elle elected not to confide in Steven due to his chattiness. When he learns of her issues, Steven's feelings are hurt, and he is disappointed he is unable to support Elle during her time of need.

Address the Issue

After talking it over with Elle, Steven understands why she refrained from sharing her issue with him. It seems as though he actually heard Elle (anyone for that matter) for the first time. "Everyone isn't an open book like you" was her response, and this time it was absorbed in a way that sparked some self-reflection. Feeling powerless to assist his friend in the manner he would have wanted during her time of need was due to his own behaviors, and it didn't sit well with him.

Elle's use of Where to Share (page 76) was a useful and even necessary aspect of her self-care plan. She didn't have the capacity to add Steven's gossiping ways to her already troublesome situation. Elle had had to abruptly gather her belongings and leave home after another verbally abusive interaction with her mother.

No longer wanting to compromise her mental health, Elle stayed in a hotel for a week until she was able to secure a short-term lease on a studio apartment. Once she had settled into her new place, Elle felt like she was ready to share her circumstances with Steven and invited him over.

Steven suggests that maybe they could become roommates once her lease is over at the end of the year so they can both save money. In the meantime, though, he wants to become more trustworthy, so Elle's going to introduce him to Where to Share (page 76).

Discussion Notes

Some friends are unconditionally trustworthy and reliable. With others, we must learn to discern at what level we can comfortably operate. Pay attention to their responses and your feelings and intuition. Do you feel free to share or guarded? When you need to act in tandem with your inner knowing or experiences, boundaries are your ally and a vital self-care tool.

Reciprocity Dilemma

Every Thursday after work, Jackson, Ahmed, and their intern, Sam, head to happy hour at the new eatery, where the prices are cheap, food is good, and drinks are plentiful. Jackson and Ahmed frequently pick up the tab, but Sam has yet to offer. It doesn't seem to bother Ahmed, who's usually just grateful to unwind from the day before returning home to his partner and twin toddlers. Jackson, on the other hand, is starting to find this pattern bothersome.

What Is Going On

Every week, Sam orders the same cheeseburger with fries and a soda. Since he doesn't drink alcohol, his portion of the check has never gone over $12. For the first three weeks, Sam offered to contribute $15 toward the tip, but Jackson and Ahmed both refused to take it, so he stopped offering. He considers these two like big brothers and simply chalks it up to the pair continuing to "look out for the college kid." With three more months until his internship with Ahmed and Jackson's firm ends, he frequently expresses his gratitude to them.

Address the Issue

Ahmed has no issue with Sam; he's just grateful for the much-needed transitional time to recharge before returning to his busy household. Transitional time is a break of sorts between tasks or responsibilities to engage in self-care through a relaxing activity and thereby avoid exhaustion, burnout, depletion, or blowing up on others. Ahmed has done his Self-Care Check-In (page 74), and his transitional time comes every Thursday.

Jackson would benefit from reflecting on why he's feeling so resentful and decide whether he'd rather accept the status quo, stop attending happy hour, or ask Sam to begin contributing. If he's feeling taken advantage of, he can find guidance in Guarding Empathy (page 60) to decide how to proceed in a way that feels right to him. The other tools within chapter 4, "Empathy," can also help Jackson view the situation from a healthier perspective. There's an opportunity to empathize with Sam being an intern and college student as well as with the fact that he had offered to cover the tip. Jackson can also do a Self-Care Check-In (page 74) and decide on happy hour. If he'd like Sam to start pitching in, hopefully he will try Assertively Advocating (page 23) so he can communicate with Sam thoughtfully and nonaggressively.

Discussion Notes

When needs or wants go unspoken, self-reflection is the gateway to meeting them. Self-reflection allows you to determine what's in your power to control and then decide how you will solve the problem. And assertive communication can help you do it in a way that respects all parties.

Possessiveness Pickle

Sinead and Conner often joke that they are one another's work spouse, and everyone knows it. Despite their banter, their friendship is platonic. They support one another and have developed a productive and successful strategy at the travel agency where they work, earning them Gold Sales Club status, the second-highest ranking at the agency. Their eyes are now set on the agency's most elite level, Platinum. Lisa, a new transfer, is excited to join their team and has thoughts on how they can reach Platinum together. Sinead and Lisa hit it off immediately, but Conner isn't happy with the change.

What Is Going On

Conner is struggling with the thought of including Lisa in his plan to achieve Platinum. It's been him and Sinead since the beginning, and he's enjoyed earning each milestone with her. He has been looking forward to finishing strong—with *her*—and Lisa disrupts the predictability he's grown accustomed to within his work environment. Given Sinead's likable demeanor, Conner isn't surprised the two bonded so quickly, but it feels weird to see his work spouse connect with someone else in a manner so similar to their connection. Lisa has encroached upon territory she didn't realize existed.

Address the Issue

Situations like this are common. People can be territorial about not only their friends but also family members, partners, or even a barber or dentist! This happens when an established relationship perceives the entry of a new person as a threat of some sort—a threat to the bond or connection, to the time shared or attention given, as it will now be divided. This can cause feelings of jealousy, territorialism, or selfishness.

Another aspect of this discomfort can be spurred by having to get to know the new person when you're already settled and comfortable with the current friendship dynamic. Conner is an introvert. For him, being around people can be draining, and the awkwardness, anxiousness, and overthinking trying to figure out somebody new can be exhausting.

Conner's rigid boundary of "no new friends" is restrictive. It limits opportunity and could stand to be relaxed. Beyond Blowing Up (page 28) can provide the reflective pause Conner needs. He can recognize that he doesn't have to be Lisa's BFF to collaborate in the interest of meeting their common goal of Platinum status (which comes with a $15,000 bonus, by the way). Sinead is his partner and friend, and that isn't going to change—their bond is solid and enduring. He has nothing to be concerned about, nothing to protect. He can then work on Adjusting Rigid Boundaries (page 53) and on accepting the new dynamic as part of his achievement plan.

Discussion Notes

Conner almost risked his opportunity to reach a lucrative goal because the journey to achieve it appeared different than he'd mapped out in his mind. Self-reflection helps guide us and keep us in check. In Conner's case, it's worth the effort to relax his boundaries. Doing so will also relax the dynamic, which may result in another rewarding and comfortable friendship.

CHAPTER 9

Work

Along with family and relationships, work is another frequently discussed topic in therapy. Jobs are stressing people out! If you count yourself among those people, this chapter has a lot of value you'll want to tap into. We'll navigate five common work-related boundary issues and combat them using tools from part 1.

Work-Life Harmony Goes MIA

While in Mexico vacationing with his family, Eric opts to remain in the villa, working through the majority of the seven-day trip. When his five-year-old son, Eric Jr., excitedly returns to share his experience watching baby sea turtles make their way to the ocean, Eric engages him but then returns to work. There's always a project, a deadline. Working during nonwork hours is a habit Eric established long ago. He has paid time off and his out-of-office responder is on, but he's still sending emails, even when adventure awaits. Eric Jr. is starting to verbally express his disappointment with Daddy missing things, and Eric Sr. is starting to feel guilty.

What Is Going On

What we have here is a classic case of *I work too damn much!* Eric is missing out on once-in-a-lifetime moments, years he'll never get back with his child. The irony here is that Eric's family is his top core value—he is letting special shared experiences slip by because he's locked into a self-imposed, inflexible work ethic that he created in the interest of providing for his family. After some reflection, Eric realizes his workaholic tendencies stem from a lingering fear of not having enough—a scarcity mindset. His inner critic tells him his efforts will never be good enough, and that's why he needs to keep working.

Address the Issue

Until he begins therapy, it would be beneficial for Eric to get back to basics and turn right to chapter 1. There he can begin by reflecting on his core values (Grounded in Knowing, page 18), then practice Cultivating Confidence (page 20), using these values as a tool to create healthy boundaries.

Though his work is demanding, Eric has more flexibility than he allows himself, and it's in his power to change. He knows he requires some self-implemented boundaries. When he takes time to think about who he is at his core, what's most important to him, and how his family wants him present in their lives, it will be clear to Eric what he needs to do.

To help create some sense of balance, Eric can use Boundaries and Self-Care (page 41) to establish how he'd like to spend his time to benefit different areas of self-care. As for his work schedule, he'd like to keep his hours to the standard workday, but if he has to work a little overtime, he can use the blocking/scheduling in Boundaries and Social Media (page 39) to segment his time, and this way he'll make sure he gets to the beach with Eric Jr. to see the sea turtles. Establishing internal work boundaries with himself will aid Eric in the true stability and sense of abundance he seeks.

Discussion Notes

Failure to rest is a societal epidemic. So many people who come to me for therapy are on a journey to improve work-life harmony. They're more stressed than ever and desperate for a healthier, more harmonious lifestyle. If you can relate, just know that we are closer than we think to the lives we desire—using tools like this can be a great first step.

Boundaries for the Entrepreneur

When Alejandro started his consulting firm with only one account two years ago, he didn't imagine it would become successful enough to replace his full-time job. But it has. With a shift to prioritizing work-life harmony, he'll transition from his corporate job to his business full-time, which will allow him to be more present with his loved ones. Alejandro has been thinking of increasing his rates for services. His hourly rate hasn't changed since he started his business, and his current rate is below market for his industry. Alejandro is somewhat concerned about his clients' potential reactions to the increase.

What Is Going On

Alejandro understands the value of the services he offers to his 45 clients. He did the research, and the rate increase is warranted. However, communicating a higher price is uncharted territory for him. He knows he'll have to be mindful of those he allows to have any form of influence on his thoughts related to business. In casual conversation, a former colleague mentioned the difficulties a friend of hers had with raising her rates and commented, "People aren't going to pay more." That statement seeped into his subconscious and diluted his confidence.

Address the Issue

Alejandro will benefit from recognizing that, as the business owner, he determines the value. He decides what his services are worth, not his clients. This can be a difficult concept for a new entrepreneur to accept, so Alejandro's first move should be Cultivating Confidence (page 20).

To strengthen his resolve and trust in himself, he can review Intuition Fruition (page 78). Alejandro already had a boundary in place with the former colleague, and he can remind himself that his intuition already steered him clear of trusting this colleague's offhand remarks. For the future, he'll benefit from deciding whom to trust by remembering Where to Share (page 76).

Once he gets past the mental hurdles, he can go on to look at the hard facts that reinforce his decision to raise his rates. Once he's feeling confident and trusting in his research (and his intuition), he can practice Assertively Advocating (page 23) to communicate the rate hike with his clients while clearly illustrating the reasoning behind it.

Discussion Notes

Your rate is your rate. Not everyone will be your client, customer, patient, or supporter. And that's OK. This doesn't just apply to entrepreneurs. In life, your aspirations are yours, and not everyone will support them. That's OK, too. When you feel hesitant about something, consider why that is. Intuition is strengthened with practice—keep practicing!

Toxic Workplace

Grace has worked in health care as a nurse administrator for 12 years. She loves what she does and believes she's living out her purpose. Because of her success with other locations, the CEO asks if she wants to take on a temporary assignment at the new Southwest location. The CEO hopes Grace will replicate what she's done at her current post and re-create the same work culture at this new one. Grace is excited about the opportunity to train and assist the recently established Southwest team. When she arrives, however, she immediately detects tension and stress among the team members.

What Is Going On

Grace can identify mismanagement from miles away and believes it has no place within a healthy work setting. She quickly realizes she's been enlisted to turn around the toxic environment that has unfortunately been established. The new unit leader started a month and a half ago and has made a mess of the department. Her style lacks flexibility and the autonomy required to foster a productive workplace. She frowns upon staff taking time off and assigns excessive caseloads, and there are reports of other poor treatment, including slights, yelling, microaggressions, and implicit bias. Clearly, this leader is the issue.

Address the Issue

Grace has two issues to address: the unit leader's mismanagement and the staff's high stress and low morale. She's reminded of the research that states, "For a sizable portion of Americans, work is demoralizing, frightening, and even traumatic" (2023 Work in America Survey, American Psychological Association).

She'll use the skills from chapter 4, "Empathy," as well as some Reflective Listening (page 48) to work through both issues. When she sits down with the staff, her empathetic and reflective listening encourage the employees to open up about the terrible working conditions. Grace must now use those skills to present the staff's concerns to the unit leader. She's doing so to make sure the manager feels heard but also so the manager can hear her own inflammatory words repeated back to her. From there, Grace will need to determine if the manager is remorseful and receptive to a performance improvement plan.

Grace will then gather the staff to discuss next steps. To help them regain some sense of satisfaction, Grace will start by hosting a mandatory staff workshop using Boundaries and Self-Care (page 41), so the staff can identify and map ways to tend to their physical, emotional, spiritual, and professional wellness going forward. The manager will be invited to join in this workshop because she, too, can use these self-care tools to her benefit as a person and a manager. Future staff workshops will focus on effectively maintaining healthy boundaries through the foundational skills in chapter 1.

Discussion Notes

In the American Psychological Association survey cited earlier, 76 percent of employees stated that working within toxic workplaces negatively impacts their mental health, resulting in anxiety, depression, and an increase in the use of alcohol, other substances, and/or food to self-soothe or self-medicate. This is why work boundaries and self-care are critical. Our lives literally depend on it.

A note to employers: In 2022, the Office of the U.S. Surgeon General created a five-point framework for employers to improve workplace mental health and well-being (see Resources, page 146).

The Saboteur

Tamera sees that Daniela purposefully withholds information from their coworker Marco. Daniela often complains to her that Marco "is a slacker and doesn't carry his weight on the team." When Marco asks Tamera about a report he hadn't received an update on, she informs him that Daniela emailed her that information a little over a week ago. Marco wonders why he didn't receive it, too, since he needs this report to complete and close out the project he's been working on. Marco reaches out to Daniela via phone to inquire if she can forward the report to him.

What Is Going On

There is an intentional breakdown in communication. Daniela has unresolved stress and feels threatened by high-achieving Marco, so she's sabotaging his ability to complete his project by withholding information he needs. When he calls her, she becomes defensive and raises her voice, stating that she has not one but two projects she is working to complete. Knowing that Daniela volunteered to take the second project on, Marco does a mental eye roll, but his tone with her does not change as he asks her again when she can send the report. When she says she's "unsure," Marco responds, "No worries," then ends the conversation and emails Tamera for the report.

Address the Issue

Several dynamics are at play here:

1. Although observant Tamera sees all kinds of interpersonal shenanigans at work, she knows her limits (Feeling for Enough, page 72) and maintains her boundaries by knowing Where to Share (page 76). She refuses to get sucked into Daniela's drama. As a reformed people pleaser, she also knows the importance of Guarding Empathy (page 60), which helps her steer clear of any issue that will sap her energy unnecessarily.

2. Daniela's current demeanor begs for several tools. She's struggling with unresolved stress and lack of self-care, so she'd benefit from a Self-Care Check-In (page 74) and some reflection on how to bring self-care into all areas of her life (Boundaries and Self-Care, page 41). Next, she might explore her core values (Grounded in Knowing, page 18) and check for alignment with her actions, and understand she has the ability to change her aggressive tone and toxic workplace behaviors using Beyond Blowing Up (page 28) and Responding Well (page 80). Ultimately, Daniela owes Marco an apology (Adjusting Rigid Boundaries, page 53). Marco is well overdue, given his tolerance and professional composure in the face of her hostility.

3. Unbeknownst to Daniela, Marco is a recovering hothead. The anger management strategies he's learned in therapy have enhanced his ability to distinguish between her issues and what doesn't belong to him. This is why he didn't blow up (Beyond Blowing Up, page 28); instead, he chose to use Assertively Advocating (page 23) by getting the report from Tamera.

Discussion Notes

What other areas do you believe should be addressed here? Are there additional tools these coworkers could apply to their situation? How would you respond to someone who appears to be sabotaging your progress or trying to impede your success? Remember that communicating and/or implementing a boundary is for you, not others. Use it to your advantage!

A Quest for Rest

Fran works part-time at a craft store and full-time as an elementary school teacher. She is a mother of four active children, one of whom is a licensed driver who can assist with her three younger siblings when she has no other commitments. Working at the craft store provides Fran with an additional source of income; plus, the employee discount allows her to purchase inexpensive supplies for her classroom and for her children's school assignments. Fran is busy teaching Monday through Friday, and her schedule at the store usually runs Monday, Tuesday, Thursday, and Saturday evenings.

What Is Going On

The only day Fran technically has "off" is Sunday, and she spends the majority of this day meal prepping, organizing, and helping the younger children get ready for their week ahead. She's noticed her energy has been low, and she can't find much time for herself. Her family and her students are her priority. When she finally falls into bed at night, she unwinds by scrolling through social media and catching up with loved ones. She loses track of time mindlessly scrolling and sending cooking reels to her younger sister. Before she realizes it, it's 2 a.m.!

Address the Issue

Many of Fran's fun weekly meal prep ideas come from recipes on Instagram, and Fran surely deserves time to relax and communicate with her sister, but she needs some boundaries for her own well-being. Boundaries and Social Media (page 39) would provide Fran with the strategy she needs to regain her good night's sleep: blocking time and adhering to a schedule. To further bolster her energy, Boundaries and Self-Care (page 41) would help Fran find ways to care for herself in all areas of life.

Although Fran likes the work she does, she could really use some support at home. She can use Assertively Advocating (page 23) to convene a family meeting and divide household responsibilities more equitably. She might discover that one of her children really wants to help with meal prep!

Discussion Notes

Those running a household often find themselves with a disproportionately heavy workload, and often, getting help is as easy as setting boundaries. Even a resistant teen is more likely to pitch in if they realize that their clothes won't clean themselves, and beginning next week, you won't be cleaning them either. Laundry lesson, tonight at 8!

CHAPTER 10

Community at Large

This chapter encompasses common issues that occur within our communities. Similar to work environments, places we frequent—like our child's school, the dentist's office, and the grocery store—are all environments where boundaries may need to be implemented as we interact with other people. Each scenario that follows will explore and solve common boundary issues that can arise in community settings.

ISSUE 21

Dismissive Doc

Joyce is in active labor, with her partner, Keith, and doula, Pam, by her side. She's taking deep breaths and swaying back and forth on a yoga ball. Joyce had decided during her first trimester on a natural birth. When her obstetrician, Dr. Thomas, arrives, she asks Joyce about her pain level and inquires if she wants any medication. Once again, Joyce reminds the doctor of her desire for a natural birth without pharmaceutical intervention.

What Is Going On

Prior to the doctor's arrival, Joyce had walked the halls and line-danced through a few contractions, with Pam twirling right alongside her while Keith recorded them. Their spirits were high in anticipation of their first child. From the first trimester of pregnancy, Joyce knew exactly what she wanted, and she had expressed this intention to her obstetrician throughout her pregnancy. Now, all these months later, her doctor is not fully respecting her wishes as she prepares to give birth. *Why did she dismiss me this way?* She is reminded of the recent spotlight on maternal mortality rates among women of African descent and the potential relationship between this statistic and implicit bias.

Address the Issue

Joyce and Keith had educated themselves and enlisted Pam, an experienced and sought-after doula, to support and guide them through pregnancy and right up to their baby's grand entrance. The mission was clear. After Dr. Thomas was reminded once again of Joyce's birth plan, there was no need to reiterate the option again unless Joyce inquired. She wouldn't, by the way. Her mind was made up.

From the doctor's perspective, she offered from a place of knowing the frequency with which other mothers have changed their minds about medications during the labor process. To Joyce, the doctor came off as dismissive and inattentive. Dr. Thomas has some work to do, by Avoiding Empathetic Failure (page 58) and enlisting some of the tools from chapter 3, "Listening to Learn."

Thankfully, Joyce is a strong woman with firm convictions. "OK, shake it off," Joyce tells herself, making a mental note to deal with *that* later. She's locked into her body and her baby; she has her team, she knows in an innate way the beautiful journey she is embarking upon, and she's ready! Her knowledge of her core values (Grounded in Knowing, page 18) and her strength in Assertively Advocating (page 23) for herself aid her in delivering a healthy baby boy, Keith-David. She is grateful to be surrounded by supporters who listened to her vision for her unique birthing experience and prioritized her needs.

Discussion Notes

A patient's expressed desire to do things their way should never be dismissed or neglected. Medical and other health care professionals take an oath to do no harm, and this includes not disregarding a patient's request. Everyone deserves to have a provider who listens, respects their needs, and provides quality care. Whether it is with your primary care physician, acupuncturist, therapist, or ophthalmologist, keep advocating as needed, and trust your instincts.

ISSUE 22

Noisy Neighbor

Newlyweds Jim and Gayle just moved into their condo in Los Angeles. Excited about starting their new lives together, they've planned their first gathering, an unpacking party with some friends. When their friends arrive, Jim opens the first box, their record player with speakers. For the occasion, he puts on some music. The friends all toast and cheer Jim and Gayle as the music plays. Within a few minutes, he hears a knock at the door. It's his new downstairs neighbor, looking very unhappy.

What Is Going On

The unhappy neighbor is the exhausted parent of a three-week-old infant, whom she was able to get to sleep just before the music began. Jim apologizes. He isn't even aware of how much noise they are making, but the neighbor is. Her colicky baby has difficulty falling asleep and staying asleep, and clearly now Mama is on the verge of tears. Jim is embarrassed to be meeting his new neighbor in such circumstances.

Address the Issue

Maintaining noise control within multi-unit living structures can become a little challenging due to the close proximity of neighbors. And moving can be a noisy task.

Being versed in Parts of Empathy (page 68), Jim empathizes with his sleep-deprived neighbor. This is not the impression he and Gayle wanted to leave on their neighbors. Jim, a recovering people pleaser, hopes the empathy he's able to express is also returned to them. Gayle comes up with an idea to give the neighbor a "we're sorry" charcuterie board. They'll need to be mindful of when to drop it off and not disturb the baby. Better yet, their neighbor might prefer that they not stop by at all as the baby's immune system is still vulnerable, and she most likely won't eat anything from neighbors she doesn't know. Together, they decide they will send a note apologizing for the disruption and offering neighborly assistance if there's anything she ever needs, plus maybe a small gift card to the gourmet coffee shop around the corner.

From the neighbor's perspective, she is fortunate to have neighbors who care so much about respecting her needs. If she had a neighbor who slammed the door on her and continued with their noisy celebration, she would need to enlist her own boundaries. Feeling for Enough (page 72) can help her disengage from future negative dealings with them. And if the inconsiderate behavior persists, perhaps it's time for the popular tool Assertively Advocating (page 23) to be used in a discussion with the building manager.

Discussion Notes

Boundaries with neighbors can be subtle or direct. Generally, thoughtful gestures, such as informing neighbors of your upcoming party and keeping nighttime noise to a minimum—and firm but polite dialogues with nosy neighbors who want to gossip or the little kid upstairs who comes over wanting to play with your dog— will help maintain smooth relations.

ISSUE 23
Know-It-All Adults

Yancy returns home from school disappointed. The 10-year-old tells her dad she's not permitted to research and present on her favorite historical figure of all time, Michael Jordan. Apparently, her teacher said Jordan hasn't made any significant contributions outside of basketball. Her dad, Marcello, smiles and shakes his head. The pair know better, as they recently took a father-daughter trip to Washington, D.C., and visited a Smithsonian museum that housed an entire section for the history-making philanthropic athlete and businessman.

What Is Going On

Teachers and educators have an extraordinary opportunity to impart knowledge to young students; conversely, one of the best gifts of teaching is a student's ability to teach the teacher as well. Teachers are in a position to nurture and ignite a student's curiosity for learning, even if it's on a topic the teacher isn't an expert on. This teacher, unaware of the facts, dismissed Yancy and missed an opportunity to learn from her student by failing to ask her about her reasons for choosing Jordan.

Address the Issue

Sometimes we teachers and educators forget that we can learn from kids! And not everyone adheres to the concept of people being lifelong learners. Some people are simply afraid of admitting they don't know everything. Others have fixed mindsets when it comes to themselves or the world around them and can make assumptions without knowing facts. When they're teachers, they can unknowingly dampen the sense of intrigue and enjoyment within the learning environment. And any adult can stunt a child's confidence and curiosity if they don't show interest in what that child has to say.

This issue might never have occurred if the teacher had simply inquired why Yancy chose this subject for her report or used Reflective Listening (page 48), which could have opened a helpful dialogue. In this case, Marcello and Yancy both used Assertively Advocating (page 23) to state their case. Marcello sent his daughter's teacher a note urging her to speak with Yancy and give her the chance to share her knowledge about Michael Jordan as a significant historical, albeit contemporary, figure. Yancy then had the opportunity to share the reasoning behind her choice of research subject. She got an A!

Discussion Notes

We all benefit from boundaries. But children may not always be able to advocate for themselves. Every adult has a responsibility to children—parents and caregivers, most of all. They are their child's number-one advocate whenever there's a need to step in and assert boundaries with somebody who is not listening, understanding, or acting in a child's best interest.

ISSUE 24

Oblivious Salesperson

Rosa's cousin's quinceañera is in a few weeks, and she still doesn't have an outfit. She heads to the mall in hopes of finding something at a boutique that's known for its high-end service and selection. Upon entering the store, she isn't initially greeted by the workers, who are deep in conversation. When one of them finally notices Rosa, she asks, "May I help you find something?" Rosa responds, "I'm trying to find a dress for a quinceañera, but I'll know it when I see it. Thank you." The salesperson nods and walks away. As Rosa begins to collect dresses, they become too heavy to carry. She looks up from the racks to find the salespeople behind the register talking again.

What Is Going On

Rosa is the only customer in this upscale store, and the service is proving to be subpar. She is frustrated and wants the dresses she's gathered to be placed in a fitting room so she can keep looking. Nobody's paying attention, so she decides to lug the dresses she has to the fitting room. She tries on the first dress but needs it in a different size, so she rings the buzzer for assistance. It takes five minutes for the sales associate to respond, and the associate seems impatient. By now Rosa is angry and feels flushed. She's tempted to leave the store.

Address the Issue

Having worked in retail, Rosa understands customer service. There's a dilemma here because although she's being ignored, the clothing options are wonderful—and she did implicitly turn away the salesperson when she said, "I'll know it when I see it."

Rosa begins to weigh the pros and cons of leaving the store empty-handed due to the poor service she's received or whether to just buy the garment and then contact corporate regarding her shopping experience. There are now two dresses that she wants to purchase, but at this point, she doesn't want either of the salespeople to earn a commission off the sale. While still in the dressing room,

Rosa takes out her phone to search for the dress online because she's reached her emotional limit (Feeling for Enough, page 72).

In the meantime, the salesperson arrives, and Rosa asks her for the dress in another size. The employee returns without the dress, explaining that the size isn't available. Rosa takes a deep breath, thanks the sales associate, and orders the dress online from another store. She might have also solved the issue by Assertively Advocating (page 23) from the start, stating that while she didn't want help finding a dress, she would appreciate assistance with bringing dresses to the dressing room and locating other sizes or similar styles. Direct, polite communication would help the salespeople more clearly understand Rosa's needs and (hopefully) assist in a more proactive way.

Discussion Notes

What would you have done if you were Rosa? If you enter a service-oriented retailer and no one greets you, are you offended? Do you continue shopping there, or do you turn around and head to another store? Or do you prefer being left alone to shop? What are your limits with this type of issue? Does it bother you, and why or why not?

Committee Martyr

Martha serves on four committees at her church. With the exception of Friday night, she facilitates or attends meetings every day of the week. She is constantly busy and lacks the time to take care of her own personal business, let alone rest. Because she is so dependable, she is often asked to take on additional administrative needs. Martha is becoming a little resentful as she questions the lack of equal distribution of tasks and committee leaders. Although she always says yes, it is starting to feel more like a heavy obligation than service from her heart.

What Is Going On

Martha says yes to every committee that needs help, and some of these committees are of little interest to her. She does so because of her faith and her desire to help her church and community, but she's not getting joy from it. She does, however, love working with the church food bank. She's coordinating the collections at the food bank for the back-to-school drive on Saturday and suddenly notices her throat is scratchy. She thinks, *I don't have time to be sick.* Saturday morning, Martha wakes up with a fever. She can barely sit up. She drifts back off to sleep and wakes up hours later to 20 missed calls.

Address the Issue

Being an active member of a community of faith can provide a tremendous sense of belonging and purpose. Although volunteering is fulfilling, we need to strike a balance. Too much is too much, no matter the environment. Martha is facing physical and spiritual burnout as she sacrifices her well-being to deliver on everything asked of her. The work she is doing has become overwhelming, and she often wants to quit it all.

Martha has served her way to sickness. The prolonged stress weakened her immune system, and now she has missed an important day serving on a committee that means the most to her.

This is exactly the push Martha needs. As she lies in bed, she reflects on her core values (Grounded in Knowing, page 18). She then draws on them to choose the two committees she loves most and will continue with going forward. Likewise, she makes a promise to herself that when she gets well, she's going to step down from the other committees. Nothing is worth risking her well-being, and she knows that with these changes, she can better serve the committees she truly cares about.

She has also decided to decline requests to assist more departments, as she simply does not have the capacity. She thinks about Boundaries and Self-Care (page 41) and decides to address these kinds of changes in all areas of her life. She's excited at the prospect of channeling her energy her way and feels her strength coming back. *Martha, honey*, she says to herself, *what took you so long?*

Discussion Notes

We can easily overextend ourselves and then wonder why we said yes to something that brings us little joy. Quality over quantity should be the priority—to serve with gladness, not begrudgingly. Through self-care and reflection, find the place where you're meant to be and don't overextend yourself. In all ways—physical, mental, emotional, and spiritual—tend to your needs.

Conclusion

You're all set. You've got the skills. The effective communication tools we introduced in part 1 and their applicability in real-life issues, such as those we explored in part 2, will continue to guide you toward establishing and maintaining healthy boundaries.

If you're still uncomfortable with the idea of setting boundaries, this is normal. Sometimes there can be feelings of anxiety, loneliness, guilt, or insecurity in telling others no and standing firm, especially when doing so is a newly acquired skill. With repetition, you'll strengthen your skills and get to a point where it will actually feel good to assert your wants and needs. I often like to compare creating new habits to strength or endurance training—it requires consistency to build muscle and stamina. It's the same with this concept: Continuous practice leads to mastery.

Knowing your values and using them to communicate assertively helps you confidently advocate for yourself in a way you can believe in. Perhaps you've learned helpful ways to get past passivity or temper aggressive responses and how clear, effective communication can be achieved through any method, including speaking, writing, emailing, and texting and via social media. You explored how listening and empathy are both closely tied to healthy communication and their ability to enhance relationships and prevent misunderstandings. Finally, everyone can benefit from emotional boundaries, so I encourage you to continue cultivating a deeper understanding of yourself and others in a way that promotes wellness and self-preservation.

While we'd all like to go through life without conflict, it happens. The scenarios presented offer solutions for all kinds of issues that commonly arise in relationships, the workplace, and our communities. Your tool bag is now filled with responses, meditations, affirmations, prompts, focal points, and exercises that can be applied to just about any situation. Whether your particular issues were illustrated or not, these skills are transferable.

Boundaries keep us healthy. They help us remain mentally fit or aid in restoring our mental fitness. Healthy boundaries keep us calm and direct us to seek rest. With them, we can avoid the pitfalls that deter us from meeting our wants and needs.

I hope this book serves as a guide that you'll frequently refer to and share with others. I also fervently hope that you always take care of yourself so you can live your life the way it was designed to be lived: Securely. With hope. With peace of mind and stability. And on your terms.

Be well and take care.

Resources

Getting Help

HEALTH IN HER HUE: Health care resources for women of color
healthinherhue.com

MELANIN AND MENTAL HEALTH: Database of therapists specializing in services for people of color
melaninandmentalhealth.com

MENTAL HEALTH AMERICA: Mental health resources including a free and confidential online mental health screening
screening.mhanational.org

NATIONAL ALLIANCE ON MENTAL ILLNESS (NAMI): National mental health organization with hundreds of local mental health affiliates and resources
nami.org

PSYCHOLOGY TODAY FIND A THERAPIST: Comprehensive therapist database for all
psychologytoday.com/us

SUBSTANCE ABUSE AND MENTAL HEALTH SERVICES ADMINISTRATION (SAMHSA): Comprehensive behavioral healthcare resources
samhsa.gov

SUICIDE AND CRISIS LIFELINE (ENGLISH OR SPANISH): 24/7 support via phone or text
Call or text 988

THERAPY FOR BLACK GIRLS: Database of therapists specializing in services for Black women and girls
providers.therapyforblackgirls.com

U.S. NATIONAL DOMESTIC VIOLENCE HOTLINE
800-799-7233

Books

Atlas of the Heart: Mapping Meaningful Connection and the Language of Human Experience by Brené Brown

The Sugar Jar: Create Boundaries, Embrace Self-Healing, and Enjoy the Sweet Things in Life by Yasmine Cheyenne

How We Heal: Uncover Power and Set Yourself Free by Alexandra Elle

Switch on Your Brain: The Key to Peak Happiness, Thinking, and Health by Caroline Leaf

Personality Plus by Florence Littauer

Set Boundaries, Find Peace: A Guide to Reclaiming Yourself by Nedra Glover Tawwab

Online Self-Care Resources

AMERICAN HORTICULTURAL THERAPY ASSOCIATION
ahta.org

TYPES AND HEALTH BENEFITS OF HYDROTHERAPY
health.clevelandclinic.org/what-is-hydrotherapy

Additional Resources

AMERICAN PSYCHOLOGICAL ASSOCIATION'S 2023 WORK IN AMERICA SURVEY: "Workplaces as Engines of Psychological Health and Well-Being"
apa.org/pubs/reports/work-in-america/2023-workplace-health-well-being

DOMESTIC ABUSE INTERVENTION PROGRAMS' POWER AND CONTROL WHEEL
theduluthmodel.org/wheels

U.S. SURGEON GENERAL'S FRAMEWORK FOR WORKPLACE MENTAL HEALTH AND WELL-BEING
hhs.gov/surgeongeneral/priorities/workplace-well-being/index.html

References

American Psychological Association. *APA Dictionary of Psychology*, 2nd ed. 2015.

Black Mamas Matter Alliance. "Key Readings." *BMMA*, October 26, 2022. https://blackmamasmatter.org/our-work/key-readings.

Brown, Brené. *Atlas of the Heart*. Penguin Random House, 2021.

Cheyenne, Yasmine. *The Sugar Jar: Create Boundaries, Embrace Self-Healing, and Enjoy the Sweet Things in Life*. Harper One, 2022.

Collins, T. J., A. Thomas, A. and E. Harris. "Unwanted and Unfollowed: Defining Ghosting and the Role of Social Media Unfollowing." *Personal Relationships 30*, no. 3 (2023): 939–59. https://doi.org/10.1111/pere.12492.

Davis, Tchiki. "9 Tips to Communicate More Assertively in Relationships." *Psychology Today*, March 6, 2023. https://www.psychologytoday.com/us/blog/click-here-for-happiness/202210/9-tips-to-communicate-more-assertively-in-relationships.

DiClemente, C. C. "Change Is a Process Not a Product: Reflections on Pieces to the Puzzle." *Substance Use & Misuse 50* (2015): 1225–28.

Dixita. "Appreciative Listening: Tips for Aspiring Leaders." *Matter*, May 7, 2021. matterapp.com/blog/appreciative-listening-tips-for-aspiring-leaders.

Drollinger, T., L. B. Comer, and P. T. Warrington, "Development and Validation of the Active Empathetic Listening Scale." *Psychology and Marketing* 23 (2006): 161–80. doi.org/10.1002=mar.20105.

Gearhart, C. C., and G. D. Bodie, "Active-Empathic Listening as a General Social Skill: Evidence from Bivariate and Canonical Correlations." *Communication Reports 24* (2011): 86–98. doi.org/10.1080/08934215.2011.610731.

Giordano, Amanda L. "Understanding the Process of Change." *Psychology Today*, October 21, 2021. psychologytoday.com/us/blog/understanding-addiction/202110/understanding-the-process-change.

Herrity, Jennifer. "How to Practice Reflective Listening (with Tips and Examples)." *Indeed*, August 15, 2024. indeed.com/career-advice/career-development/reflective-listening.

Leaf, Caroline. *Switch On Your Brain: The Key to Peak Happiness, Thinking, and Health*. Baker Books, 2013.

Littauer, Florence. *Personality Plus*. Baker Publishing Group, 1992.

Martins, Julia. "Effective Active Listening: Examples, Techniques and Exercises." *Asana*, June 21, 2024. asana.com/resources/active-listening.

Maslow, A. H. *A Theory of Human Motivation*. Martino Fine Books, 2013. Originally published in *Psychological Review 50*, no. 4 (1943): 370–96.

McLemore, Monica R., and Valentina D'Efilippo, "To Prevent Women from Dying in Childbirth, First Stop Blaming Them." *Scientific American*, May 1, 2019. scientificamerican.com/article/to-prevent-women-from-dying-in-childbirth-first-stop-blaming-them.

Minaa, B. "Three Ways You Can Take Your Boundaries Too Far—and How to Set Flexible Ones Instead." *Well+Good*, February 25, 2022. wellandgood.com/rigid-boundaries.

O'Bryan, Amanda. "How to Practice Active Listening: 16 Examples & Techniques." *Positive Psychology*, February 8, 2022. positivepsychology.com/active-listening-techniques.

Pipaș, M., and M. Jaradat, "Assertive Communication Skills." *Annales Universitatis Apulensis Series Oeconomica* 12 (2010): 649–56.

Prochaska, J. O., and C. C. DiClemente, "The Transtheoretical Approach." In *Handbook of Psychotherapy Integration*, edited by J. C. Norcross and M. R. Goldfield. Oxford University Press, 2005.

Prochaska, J. O., C. C. DiClemente, and J. C. Norcross. "In Search of How People Change: Applications to Addictive Behaviors." *American Psychologist 47* (1992): 1102–14.

Scher, S. J., and J. M. Darley, "How Effective Are the Things People Say to Apologize? Effects of the Realization of the Apology Speech Act." *Journal of Psycholinguistic Research* 26, no. 1 (1997): 127–40.

Schultz, Joshua. "How to Use Silence in Therapy and Counseling." *Positive Psychology*, April 8, 2021. positivepsychology.com/silence-in-therapy.

Six Seconds. "3 Parts of Empathy: Thoughts, Feelings, and Actions." Accessed March 19, 2024. 6seconds.org/2022/03/14/3-parts-of-empathy.

Solan, Matthew. "The Book of Neurogenesis." *Harvard Health Publishing*, August 1, 2021. health.harvard.edu/mind-and-mood/the-book-of-neurogenesis.

Steinberg, Scott. *Make Change Work for You.* TarcherPerigee, 2016.

Tawwab, Nedra Glover. *Set Boundaries, Find Peace.* Penguin Random House, 2021.

Udemy. "Five Types of Listening to Become an Awesome Listener." *Udemy.* Accessed February 5, 2024. blog.udemy.com/types-of-listening.

Whitbourne, Susan Krauss. "11 Ways That Active Listening Can Help Your Relationships." *Psychology Today*, March 13, 2012. psychologytoday.com/us/blog/fulfillment-any-age/201203/11-ways-active-listening-can-help-your-relationships.

Wood, E., L. Zivcakova, P. Gentile, K. Archer, D. De Pasquale, and A. Nosko, "Examining the Impact of Off-Task Multi-tasking with Technology on Real-Time Classroom Learning." *Computers & Education 58* (2012): 365–74. doi.org/10.1016/j.compedu.2011.08.029.

Index

Acknowledgments

TO MY FAMILY

Thank you for the love, support, and time you've provided me throughout this process. To my siblings, I love and appreciate y'all so much! Thank you for being my confidants and riding with me no matter what. MG, I can't wait to take a picture of you with this in your hands. Momma did it, Bud!

TO MY MENTORS, THERAPIST, AND THE NOURISHERS

I am grateful for the ways you've challenged me to grow, affirmed my calling, helped nurture my inner strength, and prompted me to embrace rest; not to press through but to take a break so that I won't remain broken. The advice provided during some of the most difficult and heart-wrenching times in my life while writing this book has been invaluable. You held space for me, listened and empathized without judgment, and I thank you. I believe writing this book would have been more difficult to complete without your presence along the way.

TO MY NONBIOLOGICAL SISTERS AND BROTHERS

For every prayer prayed. Positive affirmation spoken. Scripture texted, meetup just to check in, and encouraging reel sent. Thank y'all for being amazing. I am so blessed to have each of you. Much love!

TO MY BELOVED HBCUS

Dear Prairie View, you are my start, my heart, and where the seed of becoming an author was initially planted. Albeit a dissertation, Texas Southern, you're where that seed was manifested and also where a portion of this book was written. Thanks for the inspiration.

To Bailey, Tahra, Kim, and the entire Penguin Random House team, thank you for taking an unconventional encounter with me and converting it into an opportunity. Your enthusiastic support fueled me. Patty, thank you for your feedback and queries, which have further refined my skills. I am grateful to each of you.

About the Author

DR. LATOYA S. GILMORE is a licensed therapist, educator, consultant, writer, and speaker. She inspires those she works with to intentionally integrate self-care and healthy boundaries in their daily lives and is an advocate for ending the stigma related to seeking therapy.

A proud two-time HBCU graduate, Dr. Gilmore holds a bachelor's degree in psychology from Prairie View A&M University and a doctorate in counselor education from Texas Southern University. Her master's degree in marriage and family therapy was earned at Fuller Theological Seminary. Dr. Gilmore is also a member of Alpha Kappa Alpha Sorority, Inc. She's an avid tea drinker and a loyal friend who loves her family and cares for her many plant babies.

Visit lovesupportguidance.com and follow her on Instagram @dr.gilmoreshares.

Hi there,

We hope *Communication Skills for Healthier Boundaries* helped you. If you have any questions or concerns about your book, or have received a damaged copy, please contact customerservice@penguinrandomhouse.com. We're here and happy to help.

Also, please consider writing a review on your favorite retailer's website to let others know what you thought of the book.

Sincerely,

The Zeitgeist Team